SEA GRAPES AND KENNIPS

SOME OTHER PUBLICATIONS ON
VIRGIN ISLANDS HISTORY BY
ARNOLD R. HIGHFIELD

Time Longa' dan Twine
2010

·

Negotiating Enslavement
2009

·

Hans West's Accounts of St. Croix in the West Indies
2004

·

Emancipation in the U.S. Virgin Islands: 150 Years of Freedom, 1848–1998
2001

·

*J. L. Carstens' St. Thomas in Early Danish Times:
A General Description of all the Danish, American or West Indian Islands*
1997

·

St. Croix 1493: An Encounter of Two Worlds
1995

·

The Kamina Folk: Slavery and Slave Life in the Danish West Indies
1994

·

The Danish West Indian Slave Trade
(WITH GEORGE F. TYSON)
1994

·

A Caribbean Mission
1987

SEA GRAPES AND KENNIPS

The Story of Christiansted Town and Its People

ARNOLD R. HIGHFIELD

ANTILLES PRESS

2012

Copyright © 2012 Arnold R. Highfield
All rights reserved. No part of this publication may be reproduced, stored in electronic retrieval systems or transmitted by any means in any form without the prior written consent of the editors.

First printing
2012

ANTILLES PRESS
6002 Estate Diamond
Christiansted, St. Croix
United States Virgin Islands 00820

Text set in 11.5/15 Adobe Caslon
Editing by Shirley Ziegler
Typesetting, layout and cover by Paul Hoffmann
Printed in the United States of America

Second edition
Black and White Interior Edition
2016

FOR MY CHILDREN
Kevin, Leslie, Kimberly & Christopher

TABLE OF CONTENTS

Preface	ix
1. The Story of Christiansted	1
2. Government House: A Second Look	27
3. Adrian Benjamin Bentzon: Triumph & Tragedy	33
4. Lloyd "Dove" Braffith: A Genius of the Sidewalk	41
5. Will Caribs Return to Salt River?	47
6. Socha Svender & the Little Guard House	53
7. St. Croix under Which Seven Flags?	59
8. Juan Garrido: African-Iberian Conquistador & the First African on St. Croix	65
9. Antilles Airboats, Charlie, & the Goose	71
10. The University of the Virgin Islands: Our Proud Possession	77
11. Ward M. Canaday: American Industrialist & Crucian Farmer	85
12. An African Tale: Wulff Joseph Wulff, Sara Malm, & Frederik's Minde	93
13. A Danish Tale: Frederik "Africanus" Svane & Catherine Badsch	101
14. Visitors from the Sea: Cape Verde Hurricanes	109
15. Obeah, Jumbies, an' Ting	117
16. Fritz Henle: St. Croix's Master Photographer	123
17. Buccaneers, Privateers, & Pirates	131
18. Ralph D. DeChabert: Journalist, Native Leader, Gentleman	137
19. Marronage: The Flight to Freedom	143
20. Culture & Change in the Virgin Islands	149
21. Tsunamis: The Scourge of the Seas	155
22. A German West Indies?: The Brandenburgers	161
23. The Spirit of the Akan Nation in St. Croix	167

TABLE OF CONTENTS

24. Masters of Quelbe: Stanley & the Ten Sleepless Knights — 175
25. Revisiting the Columbus Landing on St. Croix,
    November 14, 1493 — 183
26. The Palestinians of St. Croix — 213
27. Crucian Danes & the Family of Charlotte Amalie Bernard — 221
28. The Virgin Islands and the Voyage of the Doomed — 233

PREFACE

THIS LITTLE volume needs scant introduction. Christiansted has been my home since 1968. As such it has never ceased to enchant me, in particular its roots that extend far back into history and pre-history. Sometimes I imagine a time before our species had set foot on these shores. In that distant age, the stretch of sand where Christiansted now stands gleamed as a magnificent two-mile stretch of brilliant beach, bordered by a bay of exquisite turquoise. And beyond that ranged a long fringing reef and a vast blue ocean to the horizon. That beach was populated by stands of Sea Grape and Kennip trees long before anyone was around to enjoy their fruit. But that isolation passed, people drifted in, and the pristine beach was suddenly transformed into a determined little town. Today, hotels, housing projects, condominiums, and businesses dominate that strand, and scarcely a Sea Grape or Kennip tree is to be seen. This collection was written in the shade of those trees in appreciation of what the place once was as well as its long evolution in becoming what it is today.

Beyond the colonial buildings, the townhouses, the government structures, and the quiet streets, Christiansted, over the years, has evolved a particular character under the impact of the various people who have come here and left their distinctive marks. In my own life here, I have spent a good deal of time tracking their footprints and their exploits. They have been a varied lot. Some chose to migrate here, some were forced to make the journey. Some came in search of the exotic, some in escape from a troubled past. For others it was the quest for paradise on earth, a place of sun, sky, and clarity. Few, it seems to me, actually found what they were seeking. But once here, they only reluctantly departed. And if they did, they always longed to come back.

SEA GRAPES AND KENNIPS

Those who pick up this book expecting a promenade through a hall of heroes will unfortunately be disappointed. On the contrary, the folks who inhabit these pages are as compelling for the compassion they inspire in their failures and faults as they are attractive for the admiration they evoke by their talents and considerable accomplishments. For my part, I have found pleasure in travelling along the same road with them for this short while, in coming to know them. I am delighted to share those pleasures with whomever might desire to accompany me for a stretch on that journey.

ACKNOWLEDGEMENTS

I would like to express my gratitude to several individuals who in one way or another contributed to the publication of this book. My brother Terry Highfield read all of the chapters and made valuable critical comments. Helen Stanbro and Lisa Spery did accurate proofreading on the final manuscript. Shirley Ziegler provided critical input to all aspects of producing the manuscript, proofreading it, and supervising its way through publication. Paul Hoffmann did all the design and layout and then shepherded the end product through the printing process with his accustomed expertise. Finally, I am indebted to my dear wife Shirley and four children—Kevin, Leslie, Kimberly, and Christopher—for their unending encouragement and love.

ARNOLD R. HIGHFIELD
St. Croix
U. S. Virgin Islands

SEA GRAPES AND KENNIPS

*The Story of Christiansted Town
and Its People*

The town of Christiansted as seen from Bülowsminde hill.

CHAPTER 1

THE STORY OF CHRISTIANSTED

INTRODUCTION

THIS PAST YEAR we have been celebrating the 275th anniversary of our town of Christiansted. That is in fact the correct commemorative date if one takes the beginning of the Danish period in St. Croix as the founding date of the town. The truth of the matter, however, is that the town is a good deal older. If the present brief sketch of the town's history is to be fully appropriate and truthful, then the discussion should begin somewhat earlier than the traditional date.

PRE-HISTORY

Although we have only scattered archaeological and inferential evidence to back up the claim of Indian settlement in pre-historic times, it is nevertheless clear that the location of present-day Christiansted was a place of settlement that extended well back into our pre-history. Archaeological evidence for this supposition in the form of artifacts is admittedly scarce. Nevertheless, there are remains near the one-time Danish battery Sophia Frederika on Protestant Cay as well as a site on the inner bay to the west of the town [Figueredo 2011]. It is altogether possible therefore that this early human presence may stretch back in time over two thousand years.

This paper was presented at The Annual Conference of The Society of Virgin Islands Historians, Government House, Christiansted, St. Croix, United States Virgin Islands, January 15, 2011.

SEA GRAPES AND KENNIPS

EARLY HISTORY

It was the onset of the Spanish conquest of the nearby Greater Antilles at the end of the fifteenth century that ultimately brought an end to the Indian habitation of the Virgin Islands. There is evidence that the last of the Island-Caribs were driven out around 1515. After their expulsion, however, Spanish forces in Puerto Rico and Santo Domingo showed no inclination to do any more in Las Islas Vírgenes than prevent other Europeans from settling there. Certainly there is no mention in any of the extant Spanish records of a permanent settlement at present-day Christiansted beyond the small groups that went there to fish and hunt turtles and perhaps undertake the construction of some rude fortifications.

In the early decades of the 17th century, the scenario of isolation began to change. Around 1630 or so, English, Dutch, and French settlers demonstrated an interest in the place. From approximately 1642 to 1645, the English and the Dutch contended for possession of the eastern half of St. Croix. For a brief time, the Dutch were at the Christiansted location but left little behind to mark their presence beyond a church. [Highfield 1995] They were driven away from the Christiansted site by a force of Spaniards after a very short stay.

By 1645, the English took possession of the entire island. A Spanish map of c.1647 shows their settlement clearly. The elements of a nascent English village were all present in our town area, including a gun battery on the point of land—today Fort Louisa Augusta—that overlooked the entrance into the bay through an opening in the fringing reef. That emplacement mounted three cannon and guarded the harbor and its modest settlement.

Just beneath the fortification and not far from the adjacent lagoon, there was a rather crude dock, directly behind which stood one of the area's larger buildings, whose function may have been that of a warehouse. A small islet in the bay, named Protestant Cay later, provided the same shelter in its lee for anchored vessels and careening activities as it provides today. The shoreline area to the south of the bay stretched

THE STORY OF CHRISTIANSTED

Spanish map of St. Croix, c.1647.

over several miles as a largely unoccupied sandy beach. And finally, on the flat plain just inland stood four large structures and nine smaller ones, bordering a road that extended from Salt River through the area toward the east end of the island. Although this tiny collection of buildings had no formal name, it was clearly the origins of a modest English village whose origins can be traced to at least 1645. The lack of significant development for this period illustrates that the island had not yet attained any real progress on the path to becoming a permanent Caribbean colony, and it soon fell victim in 1650 to Spanish arms launched from the Greater Antilles.

THE FRENCH PERIOD

Shortly after the English were evicted from St. Croix by a Spanish force in 1650, the island was seized from them by Chevalier de Poincy from his base in French St. Christopher. The French settlers called the place *Le Bourg*, or "the village." It was located on the southern shore of the reef-enclosed bay, which they called *Le Bassin*, or "the harbor." This latter term, by the way, has survived down to this day as a popular name for Christiansted. When the Danes acquired possession in

1734, they mistook the name of the harbor for the name of the town. Moreover, it was, after a time, reinterpreted by means of false etymology as "Baasend," or "Bossend," leveling over time phonologically to "Bazzen." (B*aas* was a Dutch Creole term for a Moravian Missionary, hence a "leader," or "boss.") Its meaning was re-interpreted as the "Boss End," or "capital," of the island, perhaps in juxtaposition to the name "Westend," which was employed for the later Frederiksted. Finally, it is more than likely due to the presence of several hundred illegal English settlers who had been living on St. Croix from c.1710 to 1734 that the French term was used and preferred to the new name *Christiansted*, coined by the Danes.

From a contemporary descriptive survey penned by François Blondel, Sieur des Croisettes, an eminent French Naval engineer and cartographer of the seventeenth century, there can be derived a rather elementary picture of the town of *Le Bourg*. [Blondel 1667] First, it was the focal point of shipping and commerce. Due to its location, it was considered reasonably safe from attack due to the narrow entrance through the extreme eastern end of the long, fringing reef that enclosed the broad bay.

According to some sources, the French made use of some structures left by the English, and perhaps even the earlier Dutch, namely the rudiments of a fort and a church. [Rochefort 1658] Fort St. Jean was a modest four-sided earthworks structure which overlooked the opening in the reef; it was refurbished and supplied with nine-guns in 1671. In addition, the newcomers constructed their own buildings and houses situated in the immediate area of an earthworks fort at Le Bourg; among these structures figured prominently a small weighing station called *Le Poids*. Several modest warehouses were later built by Poincy and by the French West India Company (1664–1674). As the population of the settlement gradually increased, a chapel—Nostre Dame— was constructed and maintained a short distance from the fort, the settlers being Catholic. Later, a courthouse was built to respond to the needs of justice, becoming the first administrative building. And finally,

THE STORY OF CHRISTIANSTED

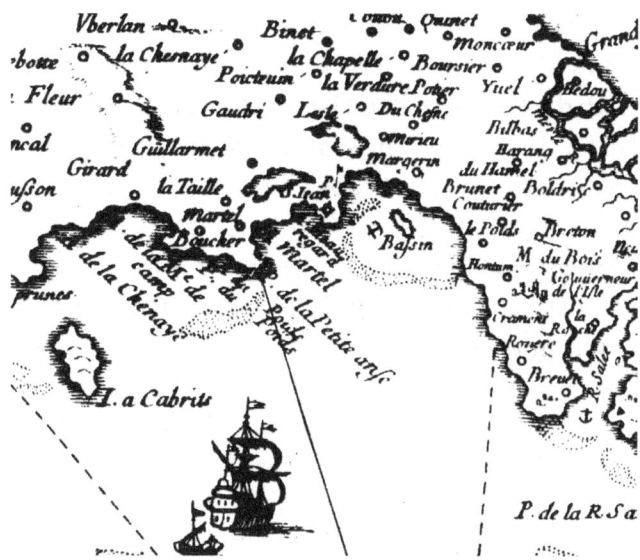

Le Bassin and Le Bourg on St. Croix, after Lapointe, 1671.

there were later a couple of rum-shops and public houses, all in all just enough to constitute a barely minimal French village.

Supply problems, war, corruption, and venality conspired to cause the French to abandon St. Croix and *Le Bourg*, its fledgling town, for St. Domingue in 1696, leaving their settlements and plantations to go back to bush. The island was subsequently visited by the itinerant French priest Père Labat in 1701, who has left us a description of a town overgrown with vine, forest, and feral livestock. [Labat 1722] For the next thirty-seven years or so, St. Croix was abandoned, claimed by France, disputed by Spain, and intermittently occupied by poor English settlers from the Leeward Islands.

DANISH WEST INDIA AND GUINEA COMPANY PERIOD, 1734–1754

The Danish West India and Guinea Company purchased St. Croix from France and took possession of the island in January 1734. Frederik Moth became the first governor (1734–1736); he later served as Governor-general of the Danish West Indies (1736–1744) in St. Thomas. He was also charged by the Directors of the Danish West India and Guinea Company with the task of undertaking a cadastral survey of the island, as well as a plan for the town of Christiansted, the former French *Le Bourg*, which was renamed in honor of King Christian VI (1730–46). [Hopkins 1987] Moth incorporated a NE-SW grid structure plan of development for the settlement and located it on his survey adjacent to the harbor.

The initial development of Christiansted at this location over its first decade was gradual but steady. The construction of a fort, Christiansvaern, on the foundation of the previous earthen French fort, was the first order of business. Some of the initial work on it, by the way, was accomplished using Africans captured from the failed rebellion on St. John of the previous year, 1733–1734. A crude drawing for that early period (*Teigning ofv. St. Croussis By*) illustrates the first structures, namely the small fort, the roads mentioned above, a church, the King's warehouse, the Danish West India and Guinea Company's warehouse, the constable's house, some slave quarters, a bakery, and some other small structures. It was a modest beginning indeed. In 1747, a Building Code for the town was authorized that provided a town plan with a distinct rectilinear design. The initial population could not have been much more than several hundred souls.

Christiansted was from the beginning the capital town of the island and the seat of administration. Moreover, it appears that it was intended from the start to become the capital of the Danish West Indies, a status that was eventually achieved in 1755. This can be laid to the Danes' expectation that St. Croix, with its flat expanses of land and its fertile soil, would become a major sugar-producing island and the bellwether of the Danish West Indies economy.

A severe hurricane struck the town in 1738 and badly damaged the fort. Work was undertaken on a new fort in that year, completed in 1749. Administrative and military offices were located there, as were the residences of the government and military officials. Christiansvaern became truly the heart and soul of the new colony and the centerpiece

THE STORY OF CHRISTIANSTED

Drawing of Christiansted, 1737.

of the town. Christiansted's first street was no doubt King Street; it connected the western entrance to the town at the later Bassin Triangle directly with the fort and the wharf. Company Street and Strand Street quickly followed, intersected by cross streets.

Religion was considered as important for a new colony as its military defenses, for the very good reason that it not only provided a response to the population's spiritual needs, but it moreover promoted good internal order and stability as well. The Lutheran Church, which was the national ecclesia of Denmark, was the first to be established. That denomination's original church, since called the Steeple Building, was constructed a short distance from Christiansvaern at the extreme eastern end of Company Street. It was followed by the Dutch Reformed Church, due to the presence of a considerable number of Dutchmen on the island, principally from St. Eustatius. In the late 1730s, the Moravians set up their Mission station in Friedensthal at the western extremity of Chistiansted, administering exclusively to the island's enslaved population. In that early period, the overwhelming majority of the island's white population was English in origin, language, and belief. St. Johns Anglican Church was therefore constructed on King Street in 1760, only to be destroyed by a hurricane in 1772, and subsequently rebuilt.

SEA GRAPES AND KENNIPS

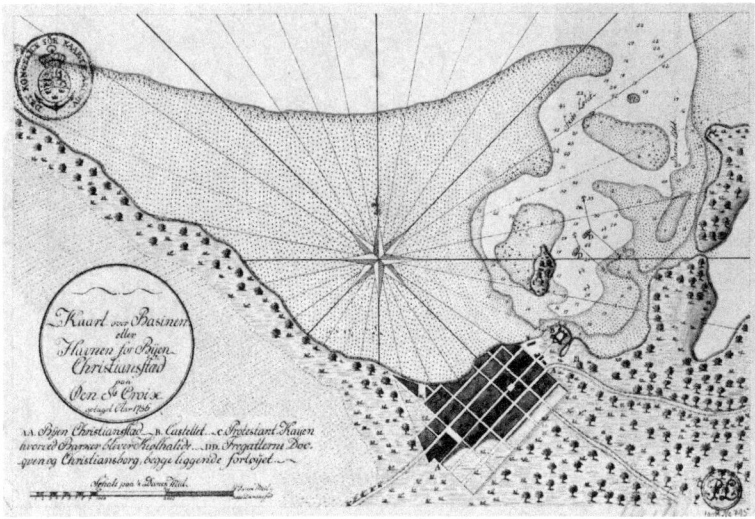

Plan of Christiansted town and the harbor, 1756 (Kraal over Basinen).

Finally, an influx of Irish and Anglo-Irish settlers occurred in the 1750s, being the occasion for the formal introduction of the Catholic faith, first at Holy Cross Church on Company Street in 1755. The island's very limited Jewish population had no synagogue but practiced its faith in meetings in private homes.

Beyond the public structures and the churches, the original private buildings were warehouses. The first of these buildings were generally two-storied affairs, with the first floor of stone masonry construction, the upper floor most often of wood, covered by imported shingles. While visiting vessels unloaded materials such as lumber, pitch, nails, barrels, and the like directly onto the dock for display and sale, other, more varied goods were packed into the first floors of warehouses, located primarily along King Street and Company Street. So it was that the bottom floors were dedicated primarily to commerce, the upper floors were often used as places of residence for the merchants, their families, and their workers. At its inception, Christiansted was a town where people both lived and worked side-by-side.

Human cargoes from Africa and from other islands in the Carib-

THE STORY OF CHRISTIANSTED

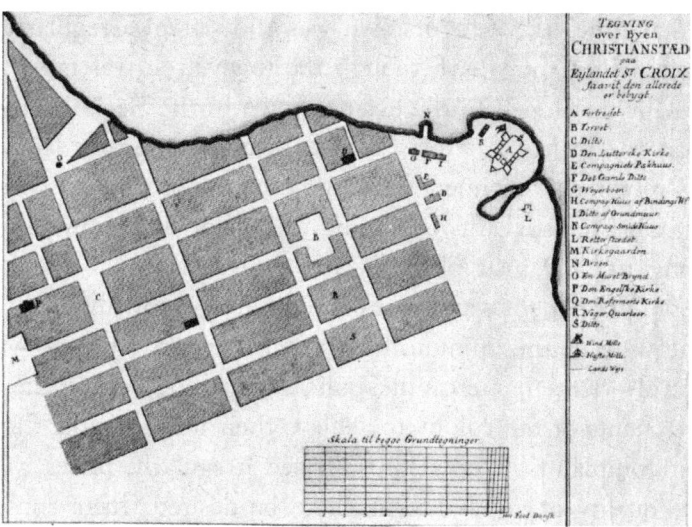

Plan of the town of Christiansted, from the Beck map, 1754.

bean also arrived on that same wharf. This trade remained a major part of the town's commerce from 1734 until it was abolished by law in 1803. [Green–Pedersen 1996] Though most of the enslaved were destined for life on the interior plantations, some of them came to reside from very early in Christiansted, as workers and domestic servants. There also appeared an intermediate class of racially mixed persons of color, some of whom gained their freedom and sought out work, trades, and residence in town as well. From the beginning their numbers matched and soon surpassed those of the Whites. Until now the African-Crucian contribution to the history of Christiansted has been either overlooked or downplayed.

The first decade of St. Croix and its principal town under the Company saw slow development. In the mid-1740s, however, that began to change—new plantations were opened, sugar production increased in significant numbers, and the population grew, all developments that had a calculable impact on Christiansted. The town plan inset on the well-known Beck map 1754 shows the greatest extent of development of the island and the town under the Danish West India Company up to that time. The view of town was laid out in a regular grid pattern, focused on the wharf, though the town itself was most probably not actually developed to the extent shown in the Beck illustration. In this plan the principal streets and markets were clearly laid out in a strictly rectilinear manner. Twenty years after the purchase from France, Christiansted was beginning to develop and grow impressively according to a Danish plan. By the 1750s, the town could boast a number of permanent warehouses and impressive townhouses.

Some were of the opinion, however, that the Company, what with its control-oriented, mercantile policies, did not permit the planters and merchants of the colony to achieve their full potential for growth. In their complaints, supply ships arrived irregularly, prices were high, and the quality of goods left much to be desired. There consequently arose considerable discontent among planters and merchants alike, who espoused the desire for a change of status to a more openly operated crown colony, with fewer restrictions and greater potential for trade. No less an authority than Adam Smith, author of the *Wealth of Nations*, has written:

> "The small islands of St. Thomas and Santa Cruz are the only countries in the new world that have ever been possessed by the Danes. These little settlements, too, were under the government of an exclusive company, which had the sole right, both of purchasing the surplus produce of the colonists, and of supplying them with such goods of other countries as they wanted, and which, therefore, both in its purchases and sales, had not only the power of oppressing them, but the greatest temptation to do so. The government of an exclusive company of merchants is, perhaps, the worst of all governments for any country whatever. It was not, however, able to stop altogether the progress of these colonies, though it rendered it more slow and languid. The late King of Denmark dissolved this company, and since that time the prosperity of these colonies has been very great." [Smith 1952: 245–246]

It was against this background that in 1754 the Danish West Indies was sold by the Company to the Danish Crown, thereby changing the rhythm, pace, and volume of the growth of the islands, and, in particular, the town of Christiansted. The key descriptive terms for this initial period were initial organization and take-off development.

CROWN COLONY, 1755–1848

After the Danish Crown assumed control over the Danish West Indies in 1755, the town grew in direct proportion to the island's rapid development as a sugar- and cotton-producing colony. Shipping passed through the town's harbor, bringing increasing amounts of trade goods from North America and Europe and carrying away the island's tropical produce. The town communicated directly with the plantations in the island's interior over ox-cart roads and with foreign ports across the surrounding seas. This, of course, stimulated secondary trade of various kinds. The result was a degree of growth that enabled Christiansted to attain the full extent of its prosperity in the half century from 1755 until the early 1800s. [Willis 1963]

By 1755, the prosperity of the island had grown to the point that Christiansted was made the capital of the Danish West Indies in that year, displacing St. Thomas. It held that distinction until 1871, when the decline of sugar and the plantation system led to economic stasis. In the mid-eighteenth century, increased economic activity and growing wealth determined that there was a need for a government house that would be commensurate with the demands of local government and administration in a period of optimistic economic expansion. The townhouse of planter Johan William Schopen on King Street near the wharf was acquired c.1768 for that purpose. A sizable investment was made in the structure to refurbish it and outfit it for its new governmental function. In 1826, the adjacent townhouse was acquired by the government from owner Johannes Søbøtker and eventually combined with the Schopen structure; it served initially as the office of the Government Secretary and as the offices of the Debt Liquidation Commission. It too was refurbished. The remodeling of the two structures into one unit, which survives in the form of our present Government House, was completed in 1832. Architecturally and aesthetically speaking, this building is doubtlessly the finest created by the Danes during their 245 year tenure in the Caribbean and remains one of the finest colonial structures in the Caribbean. [Watkins 1996]

By the end of the 18th century, Christiansted's official and administrative structures—Christiansvaern, Government House, the Customs House, the Scale House, and the major Royal Warehouse—had all been laid out and were fully functioning. The same was true of the Lutheran, Dutch Reformed, Moravian, Anglican, and Catholic churches, all constructed along the town's principal west-east axis on King and Company streets with solid architectural foundations that bespoke confidence and permanence.

In the town's development, it was the rule that streets were laid out and built façade-to-façade at a distance of some forty feet, giving the buildings an overall look of regularity and symmetry. The most prominent of these streets were lined with substantial masonry warehouses that were owned and operated by the likes of the Crugers, the Beekmans, the Kortrights, and the Lynsens from New York, as well as by the Yards and Whites from Philadelphia and by other mercantile families from the east coast of the North American colonies. In addition, a number of the wealthier planters constructed townhouses in the better locations of town, such as those of the Schopens, the Søbøtkers, the de Nullys, and the Markoes, along with other structures of note such as Bjerget, the Penthany House, the present Lutheran Parish house, and others. And finally, smaller, more modest dwellings of simple design, with wood construction, hipped roofs, and shingled exterior walls appeared, in particular, along the cross streets that proceeded up the hill beyond the original limits of the town.

This diversification of administrative, military, commercial, and residential functions led to the formation of distinctive sections, or neighborhoods, with particular identities. For example, the wharf area and the section just behind it became identified with shipping, commerce, and government. Just to the east stood American Hill with its imposing view over the entire harbor; it was destined to become the location of some of the town's finest dwellings, mansions such as Bjerget and others. Several of these still stand in isolated elegance to this day.

Along the gut that flowed down from the hills between Queen Cross Street and King Cross Street sprang up a neighborhood known as "Free Gut," the place of residence of Christiansted's growing population of Free Coloreds and Free Blacks. [Rezende 1997] The banks of a free-flowing gut were not considered to be the most desirable location for housing, and it was therefore assigned as a residential area to this emerging class of people. Its dwellings were constructed primarily of wood and were one-story in design. Hans West, the Headmaster of the Danish School Institute in the 1790s, was not overly kind in his description of that part of town and its inhabitants:

> "[They are] morally loose to such an extent that the streets where they live, in Free Gut, are marked with greater shame here than Dybensgade or Ulkegade in Copenhagen. Here [in St. Croix] that section is not only the repository of venereal diseases but also of almost all of the stolen goods imaginable. Still, these decent folk do not steal themselves, they merely hire domestics to do it. [Highfield 2004]"

Gallows Bay evolved its own distinct identity. It took its name from the location of the punishment and execution ground of the town, situated just a stone's throw to the east of Christiansvaern. From its position on a protected inlet within the larger Christiansted bay, it was ideally suited to serve as a small fishing village, what with its protected beach and a scattering of modest dwellings. In time, a fish market sprang up between the fort and the village. To this day Gallows Bay retains its identity as one of the last bastions of a true Crucian population in Christiansted.

Watergut, another sub-district of Christiansted, is located on the bay, just to the west of the main part of town in a low-lying area west and north of North Street. A principal waterway (Watergut) of the area fed by the hills behind the town enters the bay at that location. The name is attested for the late 1760s.

SEA GRAPES AND KENNIPS

The local economy of the town functioned on the activity of several small markets and a host of independent street vendors. The small, outlying plots of agricultural land produced provisions and vegetables that were carried to the town's markets on a daily and weekly basis. The regular market, or vegetable market, stood between Company Street and Queen Street on the block between King Cross and Queen Cross streets, and operated on a daily basis. Later there appeared a "Sunday Market" at the western extremity of Company Street, where slaves could carry their produce from the countryside on Sundays for sale. These two venues provided the residents of the town with much of their subsistence in the form of provisions, vegetables, fruits, poultry, meat, and charcoal. The small market alongside the fort dealt in fruits of the sea, thereby providing a significant percentage of the residents' protein needs. In addition, the street corner vendors and the tray women answered residents' taste for baked goods, sweets, and other miscellaneous merchandise, which they hawked along the sidewalks from expansive trays that they balanced on their heads. From the town's small shops of the type operated by Rachel Fawcett, Alexander Hamilton's mother, could be purchased flour, salt fish, butter, wine, salt beef and salt pork, and other victuals from North America and Europe. A cooked meal could be purchased at almost any time from any one of numerous small cook-shops, just as a shot of rum might be imbibed at one of the town's several rum-shops. Finally, there was a scattering of boarding houses that catered to visitors' needs and provided regular home-cooked meals to residents for a modest price.

Open areas dedicated to public leisure and recreation were limited. There was, of course, the bandstand and the surrounding open area on the wharf not far from the fort. Band concerts and other presentations provided the occasions for evening gatherings. A pleasant but usually closed-off courtyard lay behind government house, visible from the street. For the town's educated class, there was an Athenaeum Club, that is, a sort of private library and literary circle, whose routine was punctuated from time to time by the offerings of visiting thespians.

THE STORY OF CHRISTIANSTED

Just to the east of present New Street, Julius von Rohr (1735–1792), a prominent engineer and local naturalist, kept a botanical garden for the numerous exotic plants that he collected, a source of fascination for not a few northern Europeans. Of a semi-public nature were the numerous courtyards located behind some of the better-appointed townhouses, open to public view, at least partially, through gates that opened onto the streets. In general the town was modestly attractive but in an unostentatious, reserved manner.

By 1800, Christiansted attained its maximum population of 5,364 souls, among which figured 1,119 Whites, 1,061 Free Coloreds, and 3,184 Enslaved. [Hornby 1985] The white population consisted of government officials, administrators, military personnel, merchants, seamen, and tradesmen; they worked in the town and generally had their residences there. Some planters maintained houses in town in order that they and their families might escape the isolation and monotony of the country plantations. They staffed these dwellings with their servants, sometimes lavishly so. From the town's inception, slaves owned by the Company, as well as those owned by the King, lived and worked in Christiansted and constituted an ever-increasing element of the population. In time, both Free Colored and Free Blacks appeared in ever-greater numbers as the result of manumission, grants from their masters, and, on occasion, free birth from having a White father. Their numbers grew rapidly and in a short time came to rival those of the Whites. Masons and carpenters from this group became central to the town's building trades. Moreover, in the management of small business, they supplied the town and its residents with numerous essential goods and services of daily life. Men such as Peter Bentzon, the silversmith, Apollo Miller, the entrepreneur, Peter Tangeloe, carpenter and Free Colored leader, and numerous others played significant roles in the town's economic and social interaction. This aspect of Christiansted's development has for the most part been overlooked until recently.

The onset of the 19th century was marked by two periods of occupation by Great Britain, the first for several months in 1801 and the second in 1807, lasting for seven years. At the end of that occupation in 1815, the growth of Christiansted slowed markedly and the reasons are not difficult to identify. During the Napoleonic Wars, the Kingdom of Denmark suffered a humiliating economic catastrophe, and national confidence sagged. The question of slave labor was being called into question across Europe. Sugar prices fluctuated and the plantation system had but a short time left before it entered a precipitous decline. It is not surprising then that by the early 1820s, Christiansted suffered stagnation in its economy, experiencing only negligible developmental growth. From that time until 1848, the island and its principal town passed through its zenith and entered a long, gradual recession. The town of Christiansted escaped none of these external pressures, and over the next three decades down to Emancipation, the loss of confidence and direction had clearly begun to show.

FROM EMANCIPATION TO SALE, 1848–1917

After Emancipation, Christiansted continued in a period of decline that had started several decades earlier. Its root cause was the decline of sugar and the loss of revenues that accrued from its exportation. A diminution of commerce followed inevitably in their train. Increasingly, we hear from the home government in Denmark that the local councils are not pulling their own weight and that administrative expenses are an increasing burden on the Danish government.

St. Thomas and its magnificent harbor were facing its own problems as well. As the age of sail was followed by the age of steam power, the new means of oceanic transport meant that longer distances could be covered in single voyages, thereby reducing the need for interval stops, such as at St. Thomas. While St. Thomas did adapt to the steam age by becoming a coaling center, overall traffic nevertheless fell off. That disruption was not, however, as severe as the one suffered by St. Croix, which was in direct relation to the decline of sugar prices and, concomitantly, the failure of plantations. By the 1870s annual sugar production had fallen off by an average of about 33% while the percentage of land under cultivation had decreased from 1850 by some 22.4%, disasters by any measure. [Highfield 1983] All this occurred against the backdrop of a world depression that stretched into the 1890s. The most striking mark of the rapid decline of sugar and its effects on the Crucian economy was the transfer of the capital of the Danish islands from Christiansted in 1871 back to St. Thomas.

And as the plantations deteriorated between 1848 and 1878, so did the town, because it enjoyed no economic raison d'être beyond service to the estates and their activities. Moreover, adverse events on those estates had direct impacts on the town. When slavery came to an end in 1848, the government struggled to find a means to keep the newly freed laborers on the plantations and thereby maintain the failing sugar economy. For their part, the workers made determined efforts to escape attempts to force them to remain on the plantations in their pre-Emancipation positions. In the 1870s, the country district population fell off some 27.5%, while at the same time the population of the island's towns surged by 8.4%. Christiansted town was becoming the first stop in the workers' flight from the country plantations. [Highfield 1983]

During this same period, the town was certainly not without its share of other difficulties and the resultant hard times. After Emancipation, there occurred no little discontent and unrest, such as the Christmas disturbance in 1852, followed by the much more serious Fireburn of 1878, which sent another wave of country-dwellers into the town in search of work and shelter. Natural disasters also exacted their toll. Along with the rest of the island, the town suffered from the major hurricanes of 1853, 1867, 1871, 1878, and 1916. In 1866, a fire destroyed a good proportion of the western part of the town. Throughout the period, serious epidemics broke out, including deadly cholera in the 1850s and 1890s, while diseases such as dengue fever and leprosy remained endemic. All this occurred during a period when Denmark was neither completely willing nor able to provide the assistance that was sorely needed.

Each of these elements in its own way had a direct affect on the fortunes of Christiansted. Certainly among them, the loss of economic

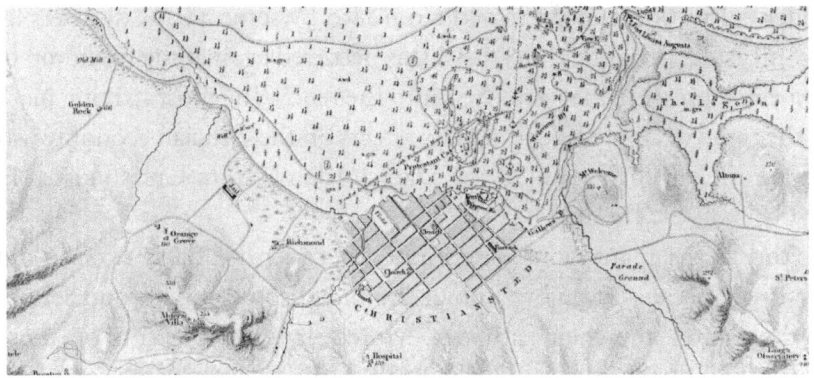

Plan of Christiansted, 1856, from Parsons.

vitality was the major reason that Denmark grew increasingly willing to sell the islands between 1867 and 1917, with Transfer ceremonies finally taking place at the Christiansted harbor on March 31, 1917. [Tansill 1932] Intimately related to this overriding issue was the rise of the first labor union and the strike of 1916, which followed from these same economic frustrations. By the time that the U.S. Navy took over, the town was in a sad state of disrepair, depression, and decline.

U.S. PERIOD, 1917–

When the U.S. assumed control in 1917, the town of Christiansted was well worn. Some problems had become engrained and chronic. The streets were unpaved; mosquito-borne diseases brought frequent sickness that the limited medical facilities could not adequately handle. Poor sewage facilities prevailed throughout the town, and public buildings were in a declining state of repair. Education beyond the bare basics was all but non-existent and underemployment was the norm. From that time to the present, the town has passed through several developmental phases that have brought further changes, both positive and negative.

NAVAL PERIOD, 1917 TO 1931

Under the authority of the U.S. Navy, some physical improvements were made, largely in the realm of basic infrastructure: health, sanitation, sewage, and education. For the most part, however, the town remained in a state of stagnation due to a lack of economic growth and to political stasis. Until 1936, the islands remained essentially under Danish colonial law. It was anything but clear exactly where the islands were heading under American ownership. The visiting President Herbert Hoover sounded an ominous note in 1931 when he characterized the islands an "effective poorhouse." [Evans 1975]

CIVILIAN RULE

At the onset of civilian rule in 1931, the Virgin Islands and Christiansted began to inch forward a little. By the end of the 1930s, some changes had occurred that would perceptibly begin to transform the character of the town, namely: New Deal programs and The Organic Act of 1936 that made possible fuller political and economic participation by locals. Moreover, the tendency toward relative economic advantage in the islands under American rule encouraged the first waves of Caribbean immigration, initially from nearby Vieques and Culebra. This movement of Hispanics began to transform the demographic profile considerably, as did, sometime later, immigration from the Eastern Caribbean islands. World War II brought greater Americanization and the gradual imposition of American values over older Danish West Indian ones, followed in the post-War period by attempts to improve the body politic (Revised Organic Act) and stimulate the economy (VICORP). [Boyer 1983] All these events pushed the island and its principal town increasingly into the American orbit.

TOURISM

But it was the advent of tourism, inspired by the charms of an 18th century Caribbean town and coupled with the growth of air travel that set things in motion toward the middle years of the twentieth century. At about that same time, in 1952, the National Park Service took over the historic wharf area with its complex of Danish colonial buildings, refurbished them, and re-oriented a significant part of Christiansted toward preservation and tourism. Gradually, the look of the town improved and visitors were attracted in ever increasing numbers. This activity signaled a need for workers in construction, hospitality, and tourism jobs, which in turn stimulated immigration from other Caribbean islands to replace the locals who were beginning to move up the economic ladder or emigrate to the United States mainland.

As the local economy grew, Christiansted faced a need for more developmental space. Suburbanization occurred suddenly in the 1960s and changed the character of things dramatically. Whereas in late Danish times the town's western boundary stood at Bassin Triangle, expansion began to move beyond that point in a westerly direction, into an area known as the "Western Suburb." Light industries, small businesses, shops, government offices, public housing, schools, public utilities, and private residences sprang up all along the North Shore road in the areas generally referred to as Richmond, Golden Rock, and Princesse. This same phenomenon also occurred to the east of the town, though on a much more limited basis, especially in the form of businesses in Gallows Bay and residential developments such as Tide Village and at Mt. Washington. In the post-war years in the 1950s and 1960s, Christiansted held steady at its historic core but grew substantially around its periphery.

INDUSTRY

In the late 1960s and 1970s, the pace quickened with the arrival of both heavy and light industry. While many of the light industries, especially the small watch assembly factories, settled in the western outskirts of the town, the heavy industries—Hess Oil and Harvey Aluminium—established their factories toward the center of the island on the south shore, with access to newly created port facilities. The same area also became the location of general port of entry for the island, which replaced the limited capacity of the harbor of Christiansted and the unprotected, open roadstead at Frederiksted. Business and residential developments also were attracted to that same sector, beginning in 1969 with the opening of the island's first large shopping center and adjacent housing complexes. Within ten years it became readily apparent that St.

Croix's economic locus was shifting away from its traditional center in Christiansted in favor of the center-island and the south shore.

SCHOOLS AND CHURCHES

It was not only in the economic sphere that the forces of development were moving inexorably toward center-island. Previously located in the towns in the early American period, the island's schools that were being created on large-scale American models, gravitated towards the wider spaces of center-island, including the newly established College of the Virgin Islands in the mid-1960s. A similar movement also occurred with respect to new churches, in particular those of the late coming Protestant Pentacostal and Fundamentalist persuasions for the most part, as well as the fairly recently established Hebrew synagogue and the Islamic mosque.

DEMOGRAPHY

During that same time frame, Crucian families that had generations earlier been attracted to Christiansted in the aftermath of slavery, began to abandon the town in increasing numbers, some for the "country," some for new lives in the U.S. mainland. Gone suddenly were the old ladies who sat by the windows on the second floors of their residences all along Company Street and King Street and surveyed their streets' activities below with appropriate commentary. A new population replaced them, largely eastern Caribbean people and, later, immigrants from the Dominican Republic. The town, with the exception of Gallows Bay, rather lost its dominant Crucian character and personality that dated back to the onset of the 19th century in exchange for the new demographic entities that have grown dominant today.

From the 1960s onward, Christiansted retained a number of its dominant features: it remained the nominal capital of the island; it maintained its appeal to tourism, especially the historic variety; restaurants, tourist shops, law firms, and realty offices continued to do business if not thrive; and the historic areas maintained by the National Park Service still projected their charms and historic interest. At the same time, however, the gradual shift away from the town has continued in the crucial areas of the economy, business, government, education, and the like, leaving the town less prominent, less central, and less important by the 1980s than it once was.

POST HUGO PROBLEMS

In September 1989, these developments were set in high relief when Christiansted was hit directly by the monster storm, Hurricane Hugo, a truly unique event in the town's long history. The town suffered catastrophic damages, followed immediately by open looting, and, in the long term, by a serious blow to the civic psyche. The repair and recovery period was slow, painful, and lacking in coherence. In fact, signs of the destruction have remained clearly visible in some parts of the town for the past twenty years. In the meantime, much of the island's post–Hugo redevelopment has simply bypassed the town, leaving it in some ways worse off than it was in 1989.

Concurrently, urban blight has raised its ugly head, creating problems of crime, violence, prostitution, drugs, and a rapid turn over in population. These problems began in the 1960s and have grown apace over the past fifty years, until the period immediately after Hurricane Hugo, when they assumed crisis proportions. Business, tourism, and the hotel industry all suffered long-term damages from the great storm and stagnated in the depressed years that followed. Virgin Island natives, for their part, accelerated their departure from the town, and neighborhoods have visibly deteriorated. But by far the greatest consideration is that Christiansted is no longer in direct connection with the internal workings of the island's economy in the same way that it once related to the plantation system but rather must rely on its own resources for direction, drive, and vitality. These enormous changes have occurred over a period during which the town has failed to develop municipal government and a degree of autonomy. To date the elements needed to move forward—municipal will, political autonomy, selfless leadership,

THE STORY OF CHRISTIANSTED

and a match of community desire with the full potential of the island and town resources—have not yet fallen into place.

FINAL NOTE

The town of Christiansted has been around for some 275 years if 1735 is taken to be the founding date. Another ninety years can be added to that span if the French and English settlements dating back to 1645 are taken into account, coming to some 365 years in all. And beyond that date, it might be safely said that the location has been the site of human habitation for some 2,500 years into the distant past, bringing our commemorative date to something on the order of 2,865 years, a rather astounding figure by any measure. These few facts demonstrate to us without equivocation that the location where we are standing today is obviously one of the special places on our planet, worthy of our esteem for its long past, equally worthy of our careful stewardship in the present and well into the future, at a time when it is dearly needed.

REFERENCES

Blondel, M. "Mémoire sur l'ile de St. Croix." 1667. Ministerie de la Marine et des Colonies. [Arch. Nat., Section O.–M., Dépôt des Fortifications des Colonies, Mémoires géneraux: Amérique méridionale et Antilles Françaises, Carton No. 1, No. d'Ordre 6, Blondel & Clodoré.]

Boyer, William W. *America's Virgin Islands. A History Of Human Rights and Wrongs.* Durham, NC: Carolina Academic Press, 1983.

Evans, Luther Harris. *The Virgin Islands from Naval Base To New Deal.* Westport, CT: Greenwood Press, 1975. [First edition: Ann Arbor, MI: J.W. Edwards, 1945.]

Figueredo, Alfredo E. "Personal communication, January 27, 2011."

Green-Pedersen, Svend E[rik]. "The Scope and Structure of the Danish Negro Slave Trade." *Bondmen And Freedmen in the Danish West*

Indies: Scholarly Perspectives. Edited by George F. Tyson. U.S. Virgin Islands: Virgin Islands Humanities Council, 1996. pp. 18–53.

Highfield, Arnold R. "The Conditions of the Working Class in the Danish West Indies in the Period 1848–1878." A chapter of a volume entitled *Freedom's Flame: Emancipation, a Second Look*. St. Croix, USVI: Bureau of Libraries, Museums and Archaeological Services, 1983. pp. 15–26.

Highfield, Arnold R. "Dutch Colonization on St. Croix in the Seventeenth Century," *Bulletin of the Society of Virgin Islands Historians* 8:1 (1995): 8–15.

Highfield, Arnold R., ed. *Hans West's Accounts of St. Croix in the West Indies*. Translation by Nina York. St. Thomas: Virgin Islands Humanities Council, 2004.

Hopkins, Daniel. "The Danish Cadastral Survey of St. Croix, 1733–1754." Doctoral Dissertation, Louisiana State University, 1987.

Hornby, Ove. "The Town of Christiansted in Danish Times," *Christiansted: 250th Anniversary, 1735–1985*. Christiansted, St. Croix: Sponsored by the Friends of Florence Williams Library and funded in part by the Virgin Islands Humanities Council, 1985. 82 pp.

Labat, Jean-Baptiste. *Nouveau Voyage aux Isles de l'Amerique*. Paris, 1722. 6 v.

Rezende, Elizabeth. "Cultural Identity of the Free Colored in Christiansted, St. Croix, Danish West Indies 1800–1848." Doctoral dissertation for The Union Institute. St. Croix, Virgin Islands, 1997.

Rochefort, César de. *Histoire naturelle et morale des iles Antilles de l'Amérique. Enrichie de plusieurs belles figures des raretez les plus considéerables qui y sont d'e écrites*. Roterdam: A. Leers, 1658.

Smith, Adam. *An Inquiry Into the Nature and Causes of the Wealth of Nations*. Chicago, IL: William Benton, Encyclopedia Britannica, 1952.

Tansill, Charles Callan. *The Purchase of the Danish West Indies.* Baltimore/London: The Johns Hopkins Press and the Oxford University Press, 1932.

Watkins, Priscilla. *Government House, St. Croix: Its History and Special Furnishings.* St. Croix: The St. Croix Landmarks Society, 1996.

Willis, Jean Louise. "The Trade Between North America and The Danish West Indies, 1756–1807, with Special Reference to St. Croix." Dissertation for Columbia University, 1963.

The eastern entrance to Government House, Christiansted, St. Croix.

CHAPTER 2

GOVERNMENT HOUSE: A SECOND LOOK

SOME THINGS IN LIFE become so routine that we walk right past them without taking notice. If I said that we have here in Christiansted perhaps the finest example of Caribbean colonial architecture still in existence, that statement might well draw a bemused yawn from not a few Crucians. I am referring, of course, to our Government House, which many of us pass on a daily basis without so much as a sideways glance of appreciation.

Government House is of course located along King Street in Christiansted, just one block from the town's wharf area and harbor. It stands three stories in height and runs to 350 feet in length and varies from 27 to 42 feet in width. There is a lovely courtyard behind the building, adorned with trees, flowers, a fountain, and walkways. The structure's light cream color, contrasted with white trim, green shutters and louvers, magnifies the Caribbean sun in all its brilliance. As such, it casts an imposing impression while at the same time remaining luminous in appearance and stately in presence. It is pleasing to the eye and responsive to our sense of proportion.

St. Croix became Danish in 1734 when it was purchased from the French by the Danish West India and Guinea Company. The motive behind the acquisition was to put the island's flat, fertile land to work in the production of sugar. That idea was a success. Fort Christiansvaern was constructed at the very beginning of the colony right at the edge of the harbor in the newly established town of Christiansted to protect the island from attack from without and slave uprisings from within. It was also intended to serve as the earliest seat of government and

SEA GRAPES AND KENNIPS

administration for the new colony. But as the economy grew and the job of governing became more complicated, the fort proved increasingly inadequate for the task at hand. This was all the more the case when the capital of the islands was moved to Christiansted in 1755, where it remained until 1871.

In 1771, the government moved to accommodate the new capital by purchasing the private mansion on King Street that had been the residence of James Schopen and his family. Schopen died that same year and his wife sold the property to the Danish West Indian government without delay. Schopen had ventured out to St. Croix in 1742 as a Company employee to seek his fortune. As a successful merchant and plantation owner, he constructed an impressive townhouse at No. 3 King Street Christiansted, which was intended to reflect his success in the colony. It was indeed an imposing structure for the time. It was in this manner that his residence became the first part of our Government House.

The second piece of the puzzle came in 1826 when the government bought the adjacent Søbøtker mansion that stood at No. 4 King St., at the corner of Queen Cross and King Streets. The new purchase was conjoined to the Schopen place in order to serve the growing need for office space and to house the Royal Debt Liquidation Commission. The remodeling required to integrate the two structures was completed in 1832 during the governorship of Peter von Scholten, and Government House began to take on its modern proportions.

Construction on the Søbøtker house had been initiated in 1794 by Adam Søbøtker. It was completed in 1797 and soon became the family's residence in Christiansted. It boasted a carriage entry on Queen Cross St., facing the eastern entrance to the Lutheran Church, and a courtyard lined the southern side with outbuildings for storage and warehousing. It was a fine complement to the family's sugar plantation at Estate Hogensborg on the western part of the island, along with other plantations that the family owned elsewhere. The sugar trade formed the base of the Søbøtker wealth and standing in the community and provided the means whereby the town mansion was constructed.

GOVERNMENT HOUSE: A SECOND LOOK

King Street view of Government House.

In terms of architectural style, both buildings were constructed in the second half of the eighteenth century at a time when fundamental changes were occurring in architecture in Denmark. In the 1750s, the prevailing Rococo style of building previously championed by master architect Nicolai Eigtved was displaced by neoclassicism imported from France. That change quickly spread throughout Denmark and soon reverberated even in the Danish colonies abroad as well, clearly visible in the façades of both the Schopen and the Søbøtker buildings even today.

It was also in the 1830s that other important changes were made to Government House. The most visible of these was the addition of the graceful pyramidal staircase at the east end of the structure leading up to an open gallery that looks over King Street and the harbor. At the same time, the Great Hall, with its polished hardwood floors, chandeliers, and mirrors along the length of the room, was created under the auspices of Governor von Scholten. It is by this latter feature of the building that Government House is best known and appreciated today by the people of the Virgin Islands.

SEA GRAPES AND KENNIPS

St. Croix's durable government House has continued to evolve and adapt down to the present time, surviving fires (1936), hurricanes (1989), and the ever present need for change. Government offices and courtrooms over the years have been moved to peripheral locations around the island, sometimes giving the stately building an impression of desertion and under-use. But its central function as the official seat of government on St. Croix, as the residence of the governor, and as the preferred site of special meetings, celebrations, and festivities assures that Government House will continue to occupy an esteemed position in the hearts and minds of Virgin Islanders for years to come.

Adrian Bentzon, 1777–1827, Governor of the Danish West Indies from 1816 to 1819.

CHAPTER 3

ADRIAN BENJAMIN BENTZON: TRIUMPH & TRAGEDY

THE VIRGIN ISLANDS has had a number of governors of exceptional talent and accomplishment in its long history. The exploits and achievements of Jørgen Iversen, Peter von Scholten, Charles Harwood, William Hastie, Ralph Paiewonsky, and Melvin Evans are well known to us all. But there are some who have passed before the eye of the historian virtually unnoticed and scarcely remarked upon. One such man was Adrian Benjamin Bentzon, who served as governor of the Danish West Indies from 1816 to 1819 and whose life of alternating triumphs and tragedies merits a closer look.

Adrian Bentzon was born at Tønsberg in Norway on April 22, 1777, where his father was a town official. Adrian completed his baccalaureate at the Latin School in the city of Bergen in 1793 and went on to the University of Copenhagen to study law. He was known among his fellow students to be serious, intelligent, and aesthetically minded. Those mental abilities were offset, at least in part, by a leg injury that plagued him from his youth.

His early life shows the marks of a literary disposition. At the university he wrote an essay on poetry that revealed a keen, penetrating mind, which earned him, in 1796, the University Gold Medal. Later, he translated from German into Danish some of the works of the popular German playwrights August von Kotzebue (1761–1819) and Friedrich Ludwig Schröder (1744–1816), this latter the dramatist who introduced Shakespeare to the German theatre. On a more personal level, he became closely acquainted with Denmark's greatest poet and dramatist of his age, Adam Gottliob Oehlenschläger (1779–1850). Had these inclinations borne early fruit, Bentzon might very well have succeeded at a career in literature and the arts.

He passed his university exams in 1797 and two years later accepted a post as Government Secretary in the colonial administration of the Danish West Indies. That position proved short-lived as the British fleet under the command of Admiral Duckworth seized the Danish islands in 1801 as a consequence of the Napoleonic Wars in Europe. Bentzon departed for North America, where he remained until after the islands had been returned to Denmark in 1802.

Over the next five years, Bentzon acquired a plantation on St. Croix and became involved in the cultivation and commerce of sugar. He also entered into a romantic relationship with a certain Henrietta Coppy, a woman of color, who bore him a daughter, Eliza Frederika Bentzon, in 1804 and a son, William Fredrik Bentzon, in 1808.

But lightning soon struck twice from the same thundercloud. In 1807, the British took possession of the Danish West Indies once again, in order to prevent the colony from possibly falling into French hands; they held those islands during that second occupation until 1815. Bentzon, though allowed to retain his property and derive profits from its cultivation, once again chose to leave St. Croix.

It was at about this same time that he met and fell in love with an attractive young woman who was taking a cruise through the islands. But she was not just any young woman. She was the daughter of a German immigrant to the United States, who was in time to become that nation's wealthiest man, John Jacob Astor (1763–1848). Magdalen Astor (1788–1832) and Adrian Bentzon exchanged vows in New York on September 14, 1807, and settled into a large house on Richmond Hill that father John Jacob had previously rented to the former New York governor and then vice-president of the United States, George Clinton. Adrian Bentzon was through this marriage inducted into the inner circle of great American wealth.

For the next seven years, until about 1814, Bentzon lived principally in the United States and made numerous trips abroad in the service of his

ADRIAN BENJAMIN BENTZON: TRIUMPH & TRAGEDY

John Jacob Astor, 1763–1848, the multi-millionaire father-in-law of Adrian Bentzon.

ambitious father-in-law. His knowledge of world affairs, his acquaintance with various world leaders (Metternich, Tallyrand, Frederik VI, and others), his talent for languages, and his charming personality gave him easy entry into international politics and big business. What a pleasant surprise it was for Astor when his son-in-law introduced him to Andrei Dashkov, the Russian Ambassador to the United States. Shortly thereafter, Astor sent Bentzon to St. Petersburg, Russia, where he negotiated a deal whereby Astor would enjoy the sole right to supply goods to the Russian territory in the northwest and also be allowed to trade in that area. From that coup came the Astor empire's penetration into the North American Northwest, Alaska, and Canada, as well as the subsequent accrual of the immense fortune that resulted from that enterprise. For a time, Bentzon was central in his father-in-law's grand adventures.

When Great Britain returned the Danish West Indian islands to Denmark in 1815 just at the close of the Napoleonic Wars and the subsequent negotiations of the Congress of Vienna, Bentzon returned to his plantations in the Danish West Indies and his former life there. In quick succession he received several honors from the Danish government, topped off by being named Governor-general of the islands in 1816. He was imminently qualified for that post by his intellectual achievements, his broad experience, his connections with eminent men of international standing, and, not least, his friendship with the Danish King, Frederik VI.

That position, however, was rife with difficulties. Denmark had only recently passed through extremely difficult economic times. Demands were being made by the Free Colored population for an expansion of their rights. The islands' slave population had grown restive during the period of British occupation, which exposed the weaknesses and limitations of Danish rule over them. And finally, there was much anxiety among the planters, many of whom were non-Danish and non-permanent residents of the island. The challenges facing Bentzon were from the start formidable.

But those constituted only some of his vexations. By all accounts Bentzon's union with the temperamental Magdalen was an unhappy one from the outset. His triumphant return to St. Croix she rendered hollow when she refused to join him there, leaving the new governor embarrassed and standing on the dock as her ship landed without her on-board. The final blow fell shortly thereafter, when their son John Jacob Bentzon died at the age of nine in a drowning accident in Washington, D.C., in the company of his grandfather. At that point, the marriage simply came apart. Magdalen divorced Bentzon in 1819 and remarried in the following year.

Bentzon's troubles continued apace. At about that same time, he became embroiled in a series of disputes with some of St. Croix's powerful plantation owners. As governor, he argued that too many of the planters lived off-island and consequently should be taxed as absentee owners. That unpopular opinion stirred up controversy, and some planters reacted with charges of peculation and other wrongdoing against him. A commission of inquiry was established, and it quickly ruled against the Governor-general. He was forced to relinquish his post in 1819. The remaining years of his life were dedicated in large part to a legal battle to clear his name, which, happily for him, occurred through a ruling of the Danish Supreme Court in 1825.

Misfortune continued to stalk Bentzon. His younger brother, Frederik Vilhelm Bentzon, died in 1826, leaving several children that he had sired with a local woman of color. Bentzon had to take on the task of their support and upbringing at a point in his life when he was little inclined or able to do so. He himself soon fell ill and was relegated to his sick-bed. His former mistress Miss Henrietta Coppy (1784–1858), herself the daughter of a Danish man, Nikolaj Coppy, and a free Mulatto woman, a certain Miss Trott, had returned to his bed and board after his divorce and remained by his side through his final trying times. His friend Hans Dahlerup reports that Bentzon consoled himself with daily reading from among some 2,500 books in German, Danish, and French that he had acquired in the final part of his life. On January 16, 1827, he passed away in quiet dignity at his home at 32 King Street in Christiansted. He was buried the next day with full military honors as reported in the *Regeringsavisen* newspaper.

Adrian Benjamin Bentzon had in effect three families during his lifetime. The first was his family (1807–1819) with Magdalen Astor that ended with the tragic death of their young son. The second was his West Indian family (1802–1827), which consisted of his two children with Henrietta Coppy. The daughter Eliza (1804–1865) of that union married Johann Hennecke, German merchant, who took her to Lower Saxony to live, where she bore him six children. She died there in 1865. The son William (1808–1853) married a woman of mixed race from St. Thomas,

SEA GRAPES AND KENNIPS

Thérèse Bentzon, 1840–1907, French writer who was Adrian Bentzon's granddaughter.

who was the daughter of a Dane, Georg Pennecke, and a woman of color, Julie Helene Pennecke, and together they raised a large family on that island.

The third family was little known until recently. In 1819–1820, on a trip to Denmark, Bentzon sojourned for a time in Paris, where he entered into a liaison with a certain Marie Virginie Clementot, said to be a dancer or actress. From that relationship a daughter was born, whom they named Olympe Bentzon. She later married a certain Baron de Vitry, and in 1840, they had a daughter, Marie Therese, who, later in life, took the name Therese Bentzon (1840–1907) in honor of her Danish grandfather. Therese went on to become the leading female writer of her time in France, publishing several well-known novels, including

Jacqueline in 1893. In this unexpected manner, it might perhaps be said that Adrian Bentzon's own previous literary aspirations were fulfilled.

The Bentzon experience is instructive of life in the Danish West Indies at that time in several respects. European men, especially those of some wealth and social standing, often maintained two families—one European and white, the other West Indian and of color. In such mixed West Indian families, the female children often went on to marry or have liaisons with European men, whereas the males of color, still bearing the stigma of race in connection with the prevailing sexual mores of the day, more often sought women of color as mates. And finally, it is clear that interracial marriage and mixing was far more extensive than present historical convention would have us believe.

Adrian Bentzon himself presents something of an enigma. His talent, ambition, good looks, and personal charm seem to have worked against him as often as not. On the one hand, he obtained a good education, acquired valued property, amassed modest wealth, and rose to admirable levels in terms of social and political position. But on the other, he twice had to leave St. Croix under duress, he committed regular adultery on his wife, lost his family through adverse conditions, suffered humiliation at the hands of his enemies, and, in the end, forfeited the political and social status for which he had struggled for so long. In the end, it might be said of him that his was a life in which the forces of a highly determined human will and a blind, impersonal destiny collided head on, leaving in the wake of this man's journey through life the irreconcilable shards of both triumph and tragedy.

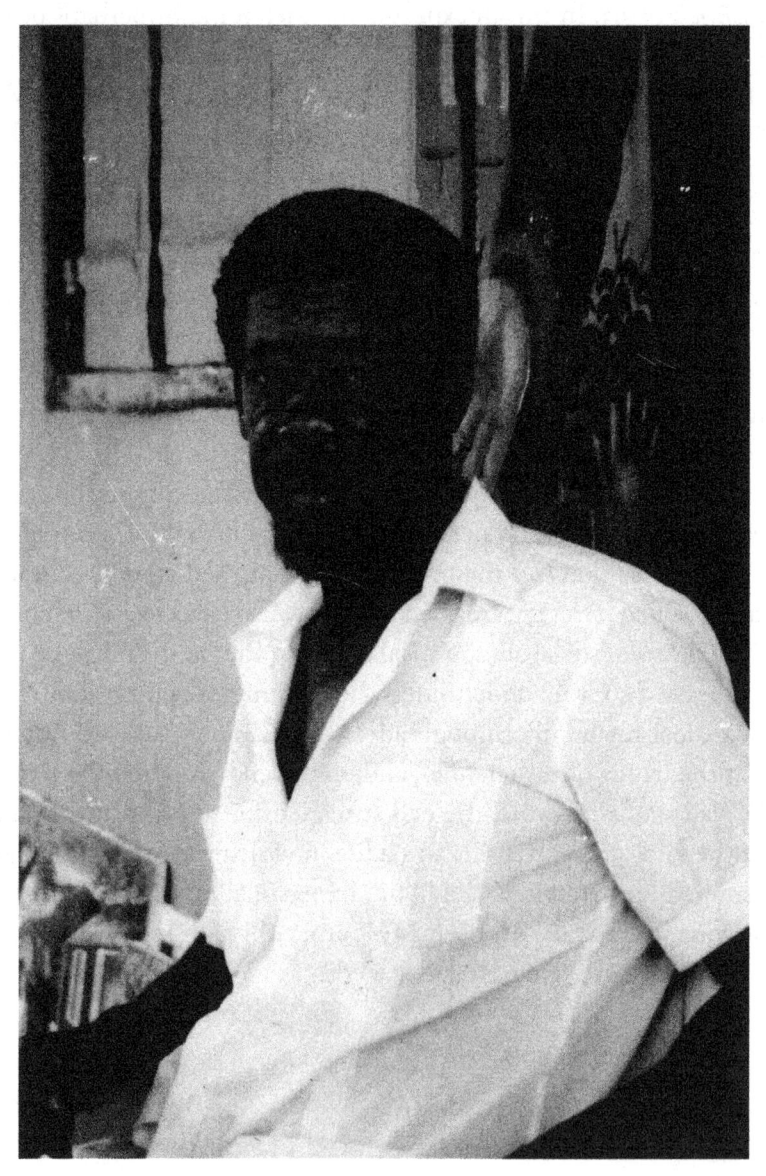

Lloyd "Dove" Braffith, 1940–2002, talented street artist on St. Croix for three decades.

CHAPTER 4

LLOYD "DOVE" BRAFFITH: A GENIUS OF THE SIDEWALK

WHEN IT COMES TIME to write the history of the twentieth century for the Virgin Islands, that story may hold a few surprises. Imagine the shock of some to learn that a man who spent most of his time inhabiting sidewalks and sitting under galleries while painting buildings and passers-by may someday be regarded as one of the seminal minds of our time. Lloyd "Dove" Braffith earned no degrees at big universities, nor did he ever amass great wealth. He wrote no important books, nor was he ever mentioned much in the newspapers. Yet he has left us some unique perspectives on how to view the world we inhabit and on choices as to how we might live life.

Anyone who ever traveled the streets of St. Croix's two towns from the 1970s through the early years of 2000 had to have crossed paths with Dove. Whether it was across the street from the Durant Castle in Frederiksted, or around Sunday Market square, or on the corner across from Holy Cross Church in Christiansted, one could not have missed him, what with his easel and brushes and acrylic paints spread out around him on the corner. And there he was, big as life, engrossed in the art of painting, completely absorbed in the act of creation. It was in this solitary act of expressing his visions of the world immediately around him that Dove transformed his talent into a vision and his life into a local institution.

Lloyd "Dove" Braffith began his life in Frederiksted in February 1940, the son of Cecelia Harris and Hezekiah Braffith. For his mother's support, Dove later expressed his deep gratitude, citing her love and the strong influence she exerted on his early development. She gave him the confidence, but where did the imagination and the focus come from?

It is difficult to say exactly when a person makes a life-changing turn. Was it, in Dove's case, when, as a youngster in grade school, he displayed a remarkable talent for drawing? Or was it the day a lady asked him to paint a sign for her? Or was it when he was asked to make a painting of the Durant Castle in Frederiksted?

Perhaps there was just something irresistible in the holding a brush up against the world, the smell of the paint as it comes into contact with the open air, something about the life-renewing effect of applying color to a lifeless surface, thereby bringing it to life, perhaps some combination of these struck Dove in a special place. However that may be, it was a short jump on his part to the realization that he could go far beyond merely applying paint to things, on the one hand, to actually breathing life into images of his own creation, on the other. In this manner, Dove the artist and the painter was born.

As a young man he had aspirations as a musician, singing calypso in a band called the "Vibrations." In 1961, he married Sherill Jackson Richardson, a union that produced three children before their divorce in 1965. In the late 1960s, he was asked to paint the Frederiksted landmark, Durant's Castle, and that initial success left a deep impression on him. Most importantly, it showed that he could actually paint. From that time on, he dedicated his life entirely to art. And interestingly enough, the Durant building was to re-appear time and again in his various paintings. He even painted the vacant lot on which the building sat after it burned down.

Dove created his finest work between the mid-seventies and the mid-nineties. During that time, he worked entirely on the streets of Frederiksted, surrounded by street people, passers-by, and the occasional admirer. When he finished a piece, he generally sold it immediately to support himself. Sometimes he worked on commission, particularly after his reputation had been established. Although he turned out pieces of real art, he seldom made enough from his work to stay

LLOYD "DOVE" BRAFFITH: A GENIUS OF THE SIDEWALK

Dove's colorful rendering of Durant Castle, in Frederiksted.

ahead of the game. He nevertheless always made it clear that he was on the street because he preferred life there.

Dove's work includes portraits, street scenes, local folks at their everyday activities, cultural events, buildings, and aerial views, especially of Frederiksted. If his portraits are few and unremarkable, the rest of his art is not. He painted locals and street scenes with considerable intimacy, drawing his inspiration from a former time, no doubt when he was young and impressionable. Though Dove lived into the twenty-first century, his artistic creation reflects earlier days that are rapidly fading before present sensibilities. It is in this manner that he affords us a look at what we were rather than what we now are and what we are becoming.

Curiously enough, it is in the aerial perspectives of the town that Dove's art has its greatest impact. I have one of these hanging in my living room, and it never ceases to attract my attention and enchant me.

SEA GRAPES AND KENNIPS

In it, Frederiksted is depicted from the south looking north over the entire town. Its arresting quality lies in the illusion that the artist seems to have elevated several hundred feet into the air and simply remained suspended there while painting the scene that spread out before him.

The unexpected perspective imbues the tableau with lightness and an unmistakable magical quality. Sunlight spills in from a setting sun in the west and exposes rich hues and colors that reflect from the rectilinear collection of Westend buildings and houses. A cluster of human figures is caught moving along an otherwise deserted street to the strains of a scratch band. One can almost feel the seductive rhythm of the distant musicians. Mocko Jumbies tower above the group, reaching out to onlookers viewing the passing scene from street-side windows. The image is complete, containing neither too little nor too much. In this one expression Dove manages to effortlessly integrate Crucians and the essence of their life-ways into the immediate ambience of the greater, surrounding world that so generously, on this occasion, embraces them. Here is sheer joy in paint.

Toward the end of the 1990s, Dove's lifestyle, reputedly given to substance abuse, took the inevitable toll on his body. Diabetes and hypertension held him firmly in their insidious grasp. In 1998, he astonished his friends and admirers in the West by moving abruptly to Christiansted, where he set up his easel under the gallery across from Holy Cross Church and then later at the corner of Company and Market streets. He once again began to paint. Dove's physical decline, however, was evident to all.

In 2002, his luck seemed to change. At that time his path was crossed by two veritable Good Samaritans. Donald and Patricia Weeden, an American couple who admired his work and artistic talent, agreed to assume all of Dove's living and painting expenses on behalf of the St. Croix Foundation in exchange for the privilege of collecting his work for an exhibition, a Dove Retrospective, the funds from which were to be used to support Dove in the future. That agreement was made in February 2002, but Dove did not live to reap the benefits from that

LLOYD "DOVE" BRAFFITH: A GENIUS OF THE SIDEWALK

arrangement. His luck ran out in November of that same year when he died suddenly from a stroke. A light quietly went out on the streets of Christiansted.

Though the passing of days is inevitable, one nevertheless regrets the inevitable change. There are times when I turn a corner and half-expect to see Dove again, seated under one of the town galleries, with his easel standing at attention before him, his eyes fixed on his latest subject. It is said that many excellent painters have come to St. Croix over the years; they painted what they saw. Dove painted only what he felt. In the doing, he left a marvelous gift to our island and to our people that is completely Crucian and completely unique.

Ernest John, Carib native from Dominica.

CHAPTER 5

WILL CARIBS RETURN TO SALT RIVER?

THE PRESENCE of African and European people in the Virgin Islands has been of relatively short duration compared with that of pre-Columbian Indian folk. Spain claimed the islands from 1493 to about 1650, interspersed with short periods of Dutch and English possession. The French held St. Croix for 83 years from 1650 to 1733, whereas Denmark maintained its West Indian colonies from 1671 down to 1917, some 246 years in all. More recently the United States has maintained these same islands as an unincorporated territory from 1917 until the present, a span of ninety-three years. These time spans pale markedly when contrasted to the approximately 3,500 years that Indian people called these islands their home.

Before we condemn the migration and invasion of European outsiders, however, we should bear in mind that the Indians too were immigrants and invaders, hop-scotching up the Lesser Antilles from the Orinoco Basin in South America in search of new habitat. They found it in many of the Caribbean islands, including St. Croix.

Three such groups are distinguishable in the pre-history of St. Croix. The first of these were the Aceramic, or Archaic people, who made no ceramics, lived by the seashores subsisting largely on marine resources, and practiced no horticulture. One archaeologist places their earliest presence here to about 3200 BCE. Faced with no real predators or enemies, they survived for nearly three millennia, until the arrival of competitors from South America around 300 BCE. Their paradise then came to an abrupt halt.

The newcomers were bearers of the Saladoid culture who spoke an

Arawakan language. On St. Croix and elsewhere nearby they discovered a home for their refined ceramics industries, their marine technology based on the canoa, their horticulture in the form of the conuco-based manioc/cassava production, and their social and political structures founded on chieftaincy, hierarchy, and status. At one time or another in that period, they occupied all of the islands of the Lesser and Greater Antilles, from Cuba to Trinidad.

Their Archaic predecessors they killed off, drove away or incorporated into their own genetic community. The net result is that the original inhabitants simply disappeared. However we may judge the newcomers, the fact is that they evolved into the more advanced Taino culture that was securely established in Hispaniola and in the other islands of the Greater Antilles in 1492 when Columbus arrived.

Not long before the coming of Admiral of the Ocean Sea at the head of an Iberian invasion, another ethnic group entered the Caribbean near Trinidad. These Cariban-speaking people made their way up through the Lesser Antilles, displacing the populations they encountered along

A carbet on Dominica.

the way. Their forward progress ended circa 1490 in and around the Virgin Islands just to the east of Taino-dominated Boriquen (Puerto Rico). These energetic invaders called themselves "Kalina," or "Kalinago," though they were later named by Columbus and the Spaniards as "Caribs," a name that stuck.

These were warrior folk who were willing to take on any and all opponents—Tainos, Spaniards, and every other stripe of European—asking no quarter and giving none in return. In the 16th century, they refused to submit to Spanish domination but rather posed a considerable threat to Spanish settlements in the West Indies, especially those in Puerto Rico. The sight of a squadron of Carib war canoas slashing across the sea inspired mortal fear in the hearts of many a Spaniard. Gradually, however, the superior fire-power and the large sailing vessels of the several European nations forced them off the high seas and into interior mountain redoubts on several islands, principally Dominica. There they have miraculously survived for several centuries down to the present, their numbers reduced but their pride intact.

Ernest John is one such Carib who recently came back to St. Croix. Born on the Carib Reserve in eastern Dominica, he grew up in the ancient Carib lifestyle but decided at an early age to "roam the world." In time he found his way to our island and, like so many others, soon discovered that it was difficult to leave. But it was equally difficult to forget Dominica and his Carib past. "I am a proud Kalinago from Waitukabuli (Dominica)," he says often, with obvious enthusiasm and pride.

Talk with him long enough and you will soon learn how a modern Carib man views the world, namely that he is torn between the inevitable attractions of the present and the irresistible lure of the past. He relates that he has for a long time tried to strike a compromise between those two forces by establishing a Carib village on St. Croix, replete with thatched carbets, war canoas, and traditional gardens, or conucos. But that road has been rocky, and to date his dreams remain just that.

One afternoon this month, we talked about his plans to organize a visit to St. Croix by some of Dominica's pure Kalinagos. But it would be, he says, "no ordinary visit." He would like to load up a dozen or so Carib canoas with his people and have them come island-hopping all the way to Salt River, the location of their first encounter with Columbus and Europeans in 1493. On the banks of that estuary or nearby, they would beach their vessels and step ashore with plans to build a traditional Carib village, plant gardens, fish the surrounding waters, and play their music and dance their dances, all aimed at demonstrating to the people of our island and to the world that they are still alive and well and determined to survive as a people. In that way, he says with a broad smile, "we would have the last word on Columbus."

It would indeed be a delight to see a dozen Carib war canoas cutting through the waters of the Buck Island Channel, hustling toward a Salt River destination. Such a fleet would provide living proof that a people who have been beaten down by the world and all but written off as an ethnic group, could, given the right balance of energy, tenacity, and sheer willpower, survive and even flourish against impossible odds.

Socha Svender, 1919–1984, German-born artist who made St. Croix her home.

CHAPTER 6

SOCHA SVENDER & THE LITTLE GUARD HOUSE

ST. CROIX and the other Virgin Islands have always been places where well-known people have come and gone over the years and continue to do so. Alexander Hamilton, Denmark Vesey, Judah Benjamin, Roy Innis, Casper Holstein, Kelsey Grammar, Tim Duncan, and others, all, for one reason or another, left these shores. Phillip Freneau, Fritz Henle, Robert Oppenheimer, William Hastie, Maureen O'Hara, and others, on the other hand, found these isles attractive and decided to come here, some of them to stay. Both of these lists could be extended considerably with names perhaps less known but with ambitions no less compelling. One such name among those who came to stay is that of Socha Svender.

My path crossed with Socha's in 1963, the year that I first set foot on St. Croix. That was before development had come to the island, before the refinery and factories, before shopping centers, a time when Christiansted was a slow-moving West Indian town, set beside an incomparable turquoise harbor. If you remember Rassmussen's Market, Harry's Office Bar, Carib Cellars, Pivar Realty, Café de Paris, The Mahoney Place, and Caron's, then you remember the time of which I speak. And let us not forget the Little Guard House.

That small shop was located on Company Street, just across from the Apothecary Hall, a delightful little place that offered a variety of wares of one kind or another—pieces of sculpture, paintings, various objets d'art, delightful dioramas, antiques, and most of all, stylish wood carvings. Socha Svender and her husband Michael were the owners. That first encounter with them was marked by two observations. How could, first of all, a person as delicate as Socha create such powerful carvings in such very hard woods? And the second was: how had people so different and seemingly unique as the two of them found their way to Christiansted? It is unfortunate that fifty years had to pass before I actually got answers to these questions.

Socha was born Sophia on April 1, 1919, in Berlin, the daughter of the Polish-born Bogdan Lackner and a French mother, Adéle Michaëlis. It was the family Nanny who bestowed the name "Sochinka" on her (later Socha, pronounced "so ha"). From the very beginning of her life, she showed a marked predilection for art. Animals fascinated her from the start, and it enchanted her to sketch them. After reading Albert Schweitzer's books on Africa a little later, she found herself drawn ever increasingly to tropical areas and to tropical people.

As a young woman in 1937, she studied painting with Max Dungert in Berlin. In time she became acquainted with Karl Schwitters, Max Pechstein, and Georg Grosz, all well-known artists in Germany at that time. But in the late 1930s, politics in the form of Nazism was catching up with German art, forcing many of the country's most accomplished artists to leave their homeland. In 1939, Socha joined the exodus and traveled to Cortina d'Ampezzo in Italy to study sculpture. There she added the third dimension of her art, and from that time sculpture was to dominate the rest of her career.

Socha was of a delicate physical constitution all of her life. It was in Italy that she began to suffer pulmonary problems. Moreover, Hitler seized power in Germany as had Mussolini in Italy, and the threats from both fascist states were beginning to shut Europe down. Socha made her way over the Alps into neutral Switzerland and found refuge in Davos, an alpine retreat long known for its treatment of pulmonary afflictions of the kind from which Socha suffered. She met Michael Svender while at the sanatorium, married him, and the two spent the duration of World War Two there in the Swiss mountains, in security but also in artistic isolation.

At the War's end, the couple made their way in 1946 to New York, where they found jobs and worked for a time. But something was lacking—light, color, life. They made trips in search of a "special place" for themselves. One such trip of exploration took them to the American southwest and Mexico, but in spite of the brilliant desert colors, their artistic spirits still went wanting. By chance, Socha came across a photo of St. Croix, and it was love at first sight. She later wrote; "When we first arrived in St. Croix, the island was a profusion of wild colors: burnt orange, golden yellow, deep purple." They had finally found their place in the world.

A new life opened up for Socha and Michael in St. Croix. They were fortunate to find friendship and a generous welcome from Ted and Betty Dale at their dramatic residence at Pull Point. Soon they made friends of all kinds. They opened their antique shop in Christiansted, which quickly became a success. And most of all, Socha's artistic life stepped into an altogether new dimension when she discovered the potential of wood from St. Croix's forests and driftwood from its beaches as a medium, as well as from the beauty and power in the faces of our people. Here the newcomers were destined to spend the rest of their lives.

Socha grew particularly fond of finding and working with local hardwoods—mahogany, Spanish cedar, and lignum vitae in particular—as well as the large pieces of driftwood, that washed up on the island's beaches. Faced with the silence of those odd pieces of wood with their curious shapes and sizes, she possessed the gift of being able to see figures and forms in her material, perhaps asleep and distant, but nevertheless there, waiting to be liberated by just the right eye, guiding just the right chisel. And liberate them she did. A few of these have been included in this article to give some idea of the measure of her talent.

The greater part of her work can be divided between portrayal of heads and bodies of both women and men from this region. Her female figures are marked by a fullness of flesh, especially in the faces, that dominates all else with their sensuousness. Her males appear older, more contemplative, silently locked in the mystery of a quest for knowledge and wisdom. In form, her rendering of the genders travels just to the

Superb Socha Svender wood statue entitled "Devoted Bride."

point of exaggeration and then pulls back, sealed with a strong measure of empathy.

Socha induced other fascinating creatures to emerge from mahogany trunks and lignum vitae limbs as well. In the course of her twenty-odd-year career on St. Croix, she produced literally hundreds of masterful carvings, which drew collectors and agents from as far as London, Paris, New York, and other art centers. Her talent having been exposed to the world, she became well-known and, if not wealthy, at least comfortable.

Time has a nasty little way of closing in on us all. Socha's weak constitution made her a particularly vulnerable target. In the 1970s, her hands became increasingly frail, no longer able to bring her chisel to entice the wood to her wishes. Her favorite material, lignum vitae, proved particularly resistant to her attempts to force fascinating faces and bodies to leap from its grain. In time, she had no choice but to lay aside her magical chisels once and for all. Indomitable spirit, however, is the expression that best describes her, for during her inevitable decline, she turned to the painter's brush and continued to draw out art from the world all around her.

In the late 1970s, Socha and her ailing husband Michael had no choice but to close down the Little Guard House permanently. Most of her carvings and paintings were sold to collectors overseas. The shop on Company Street stood empty of its marvels and was finally locked up. Cruelest of all, the place was soon leased out as a bar and the Little Guard House was no more. It was almost as if the artistic interlude had never happened at all.

Michael Svender fell ill and died in 1981. Socha followed quickly after him on August 8, 1984, in the wake of several debilitating years. A group of friends whom she had made over three decades in St. Croix, gathered on the wharf in Christiansted several days after her passing to say farewell to the delicate little woman who had spoken so powerfully through the wood that she had always loved. Her remains were slid to rest into the deep beyond the harbor reef.

What to make of her life? She said it best herself when she spoke of her last artistic creation, a piece called the "Scream," to which she applied her trembling and numb hands for six months. She characterized it as a "scream to the heavens." To that she added, that although "my life had been plagued by pain, I was happy being me. It was a wonderful life."

Some of those who come to this island only take. Some leave very little behind. Some leave themselves and their gifts completely and entirely. Socha Svender was of the latter variety.

Virgin Islands flag.

CHAPTER 7

ST. CROIX UNDER WHICH SEVEN FLAGS?

SEEING SOMETHING IN WRITING sometimes lends verisimilitude where it has no rightful place. Once a student brought me several pages copied from a book that made outrageous claims. "See, here," he chimed. "It's right here in writing so it's got to be true." There can be no doubt about it, the printed word has a special power. Once something has been committed to print, the effects can be long-lasting even when erroneous.

Something along these lines has occurred relative to St. Croix and the flags that have flown over it. When the Danes were here, they made little fuss over their island's past. As far as they were concerned it was all theirs. They flew the Danish flag over St. Croix from 1734 until 1917, and that was pretty much the end of it. When the Americans arrived, however, they were much captivated by the island's storied colonial past, which many considered exotic, even romantic. And since the island's economy soon came to depend on tourism, the idea of "St. Croix under Seven Flags" was a natural.

It was not long before the phrase "under seven flags" began to pop up just about everywhere. In 1970, great credibility was given to that expression when noted historian Florence Lewisohn published her history of the island under the title, *St. Croix under Seven Flags* (1970). In that book she did not include images of the flags themselves, but she did employ them in her extremely popular little book entitled *The Romantic History of St. Croix*, published six years previously, in 1964. In the intervening forty-odd years those words have found a permanent place in the Crucian imagination and vocabulary. And if you would like to see

SEA GRAPES AND KENNIPS

the flags in living color, make a quick pass through Sunny Isle Shopping Center, where those seven banners float daily in the breeze. It is unfortunate that some of those same flags are incorrectly represented.

Spain was the first of the seven countries to claim St. Croix. It did so from 1493, when they named it Santa Cruz (Holy Cross), holding it until 1650, when a Spanish garrison was ousted by Frenchmen under the command of Chevalier de Poincy in St. Christopher. During that 157-year stretch, Spain never settled Santa Cruz but claimed it under Spanish sovereignty and the Spanish flag, which at that time was the Cross of Burgundy. This remained the official flag of the Spanish monarchs from 1506 until 1701. Interestingly enough, this same Cross of Burgundy still flies today over Fort San Cristóbal in Puerto Rico, alongside the United States and Puerto Rican flags, in memory of the period of Spanish rule there.

The Cross of Burgundy.

The Netherlands came next, when merchants from Zeeland made a determined attempt from the 1630s to 1645 to grab the island from under the noses of the Spaniards. As the present Netherlands tricolor was officially adopted only in 1937, those early Dutchmen must have then been flying another standard. Most likely it was that of the Province of Zeeland in the Netherlands, from which most of the settlers and their leaders hailed. The earliest of the Zeeland flags of which we have knowledge dates from the late seventeenth century. It was a red-white-blue tricolor, with an extra wide white stripe, sometimes inset with the Zeeland coat of arms. Although it resembled the later Dutch tricolor of 1937, it was, however, a distinctly different flag.

Flag of Zeeland.

· 60 ·

ST. CROIX UNDER WHICH SEVEN FLAGS?

The English struggled with the Dutch for control of Santa Cruz in the early 1640s and then finally seized it and held it from 1645 to 1650, when they were driven out by resurgent Spaniards. They came very close indeed to establishing a permanent colony here. The flag they flew was the well known Union Flag, adopted in 1606, just after King James of Scotland came to the English Throne, uniting those two kingdoms. This flag consisted of the Cross of St. George (England), superimposed over the Cross of St. Andrew (Scotland), against a field of blue. It was this form of the evolving British flag that no doubt flew over Santa Cruz, not the later Union Jack that was adopted in 1801, at which time the cross of St. Patrick (Ireland) was added.

The Union Jack.

France snatched Santa Cruz from Spain in 1650 and renamed the island Sainte Croix. At that time, the white flag had been the standard of the Kings of France since late medieval times. In time, the *fleur-de-lis* (the lily flower) came to be added by the ruling Bourbon monarchs. By the time of Louis IV (1643–1715) and the French colony on Saint-Croix, the flag that flew over the island was most likely that of the *fleur-de-lis* over a white background. The well known tricolor (vertical bars of blue-white-red) came into existence only in 1794 at the onset of the French Revolution.

The French Fleur-de-lis.

In a strange twist of fate, the conqueror of Santa Cruz, Chevalier de Poincy, abruptly transferred all of his West Indian possessions—of which Sainte-Croix was only one—into the holdings of the Order of Malta in 1653, an arrangement that lasted until 1664. During that time, Sainte Croix was nominally, though not

Sovereign Order of Malta.

effectively, under the Order. Though there were few knights who ever ventured to Sainte Croix, the island was nevertheless under the rule of the Order and can be said to have been under that flag. Lacking illustrations of Sainte-Croix for that period, we will probably never know if the flag ever actually flew over any of the forts. The design of that flag was simply a white, pointed Maltese cross on a red field. It was also known as the flag of the Order's leader, the Grandmaster.

In 1734, Denmark purchased the island of Sainte Croix from France and retained it for 183 years until it was sold in 1917 to the United States. Denmark has two interesting flags—Dannebrog, a white Scandinavian cross on a red background and the Splitflag, that is, a swallowtail cut with the same cross motif. A number of illustrations from the early period show the Danish Splitflag flying over Fort Christiansvaern in Christiansted and Fort Christian on St. Thomas, just as it flew over Fort Christiansborg on the Gold Coast of Africa. So it can be said that while the Danish West Indies was definitely *under* Dannebrog and the Danish sovereignty that it represented as were other Danish lands, its most important official structures—its forts—flew the Splitflag. This was perhaps because trade vessels plying the waters to the West Indies were allowed to fly the Splitflag whereas other vessels were not.

The Danish Splitflag.

On March 30, 1917, the colors of Denmark were struck in the Virgin Islands, and the Stars and Strips—Old Glory—was raised as the islands changed hands. But that was not quite the same American flag that flies over our island today. The flag that was raised over the Virgin Islands in 1917 was at that time of recent vintage, having been created in 1912 on the admission of two new states to the Union—Arizona and New Mexico. At that time there were only forty-eight states in the Union and therefore forty-eight stars on the banner. The present flag still has the original thirteen stripes but has added two stars for Hawaii and Alaska, bringing the total to fifty.

U.S. Flag with forty-eight stars.

Sadly enough, the existing flag of the U.S. Virgin Islands has been overlooked in our obsession with the mystical number seven. But on the other hand, how would "St. Croix under eight flags" sound? All would agree, I think, that it lacks a little something. But eight it is.

Our present Territorial flag—the eighth one—is a white background, inset with a golden eagle, whose spread talons grasp three arrows on the left and an olive branch on the right. Clearly, it was calqued on the Seal of the President of the United States, no doubt to show the relationship of the islands' government to executive power. It is thought that the three arrows represent the three major islands—St. Croix, St. John, and St. Thomas.

Our present flag was adopted in 1921, while the islands were still under Naval rule, in a period before the First Organic Act (1936). That was a time when the local population had little say in anything. In that regard it is the flag that the U.S. government imposed on the islands and not the flag that the people might have chosen for themselves. While it has served its purpose well over the past century, perhaps now is the time to begin thinking about a flag that might better express the aspirations, culture, and self-image of the people of the Virgin Islands. After all, flags evolve and change naturally and fairly often over time in response to changing realities in their political lives. The U.S. flag, in fact, has undergone twenty-eight permutations since it was first adopted in 1775. So why not here?

Juan Garrido with Hernán Cortés.

CHAPTER 8

JUAN GARRIDO: AFRICAN-IBERIAN CONQUISTADOR & THE FIRST AFRICAN ON ST. CROIX

THE COLLISION of Africa and Europe in the fifteenth century had many unforeseen consequences. It is, of course, a well-known story of how numerous Africans were transported to the New World. A less well-known account is that of those Africans who made their first stop in Europe and from there advanced into the Western Hemisphere. The life of Juan Garrido is one such story.

Juan Garrido was born on the coast of West Africa sometime around 1480. At the tender age of fifteen, he traveled to Lisbon, Portugal, as a free man, which suggests that he was perhaps of royal or noble background. Portugal was one of the first European nations to embrace slave labor from Africa, importing the first Africans in 1441 and establishing a slave market in the port town of Lagos in 1444. The impact of the importation was considerable. By 1555, slaves came to make up as much as ten percent of the total population of the capital city of Lisbon. Garrido therefore entered a nation in the process of great change.

There he converted to Christianity and received a Portuguese education. Shortly thereafter, he relocated to Seville in southern Spain, at that time a city on the verge of monumental development. It was through that city on the Guadalquivir River that all merchandise exported to or imported from the Spanish Empire in the New World was obliged to pass, thereby creating wealth and limitless opportunity. Garrido managed to take advantage of that situation and cast his lot in the westward expansion. In 1502, he secured passage across the Atlantic to Hispaniola

SEA GRAPES AND KENNIPS

The Azcatitlan Codex.

with the same fleet that carried the newly appointed governor of the new venture, Nicolas de Ovando (1460–1518).

The information that follows is taken largely from Garrido's subsequent *probanza*, or petition, sent near the end of his life to King Charles as testimony of his loyal service to the Spanish Crown, in hopes of snaring a pension. It is a short but most revealing document that provides the details of Garrido's life.

Hispaniola, the island home of present-day Haiti and the Dominican Republic, was at that time teeming with adventurers in pursuit of land, Indian slaves, gold, and wealth. In 1508, Garrido joined the forces of one such man, Ponce de León (1474–1521), following him in military service, first to Boriquen (Puerto Rico) and later to other islands.

In Puerto Rico, Ponce put down Taíno resistance in 1508, founded the first Spanish town at Caparra, and in recompense became governor of the new colony. When Indian resistance continued, in particular from

JUAN GARRIDO: AFRICAN-IBERIAN CONQUISTADOR

the Caribs of the Eastern Caribbean islands, Ponce pursued them all the way to Guadeloupe and Dominica. En route, he stopped at St. Croix and reported back to the Crown that all the Indians had been removed from that island. Juan Garrido took part in all these adventures, becoming in the process the first known African to set foot on St. Croix.

Political intrigues caused Ponce to turn his attention elsewhere, drawn, it is said, by stories of the fabled Bimini and the Fountain of Youth. In 1513 and 1521, he made voyages of discovery and settlement to Florida, with Garrido and other of his conquistadores in his train. On the second voyage, Ponce was felled by a poisoned arrow and died shortly after his fleet landed in Cuba.

Garrido's presence in Cuba at that time positioned him to take part in the next big wave of Spanish expansion, the invasion and conquest of Mexico, led by Hernán Cortés in 1519. Together they fought their way inland against the more numerous Aztecs and in 1521, subdued the capital city of Tenochtitlán. After the furious battles, it was Garrido who gathered the remains of his fallen Spanish companions and buried them in the Chapel of Tacuba, called *Los Mártires* (The Martyrs) that he constructed in 1524 near the city gates.

It was during this same time that Garrido became the first Spaniard in the New World to sow and cultivate wheat, on his own plantation. In his *probanza* he relates: "In all these ways for thirty years have I served and continue to serve Your Majesty—for these reasons stated above do I petition Your Mercy. And also because I was the first to have the inspiration to sow maize here in New Spain and to see if it took; I did this and experimented at my own expense." For this gift to Mexico, Garrido was honored in the twentieth century by the Mexican painter Diego Rivera in a grand mural on the wall of the Presidential Palace in Mexico City.

Over the next eleven years or so, Garrido followed Cortés on a number of expeditions to subdue and exploit the interior of the Aztec empire in Mexico. In 1524, he was sent by Cortés along with several other conquistadores to explore the rich region of Michoacán. On his return to the capital with important information, he was rewarded by being named *portero* of the city council by Cortés. A short time later that same council named him the guardian of the aqueduct through which the city's water supply flowed from Chapultepec. For these two jobs he received eighty gold pesos per year. In addition, he continued to maintain the Chapel of the Martyrs at the city gate. During those years his military service paid a bountiful reward.

In 1527, Garrido left Tenochtitlán for Michoacán where gold was discovered. There, he tested his mettle. However, his luck quickly began to turn. He ran up unsustainable debts as a result of the purchase of both Indian and African slaves for the purpose of extracting gold from the earth. In the following year, he returned to his farm near the capital city, and there he remained for a time, engaged in agriculture for the next five years in the company of his wife and children.

Garrido found it impossible, however, to resist the call of his captain and protector, Hernán Cortés, when, in 1532, the indomitable Marques del Valle launched an expedition to an island in the Pacific then called California. It later became clear that the island was in fact the peninsula that came to be called Baja California. The hopes of conquest and riches soon proved to be illusory as the invaders suffered hunger and hardship, which forced them to give up their quest in 1535.

Garrido soon found himself impoverished, with only his farm to sustain him. Age was upon him, his income was severely diminished, and the last major expedition by his protector-captain Hernán Cortés took place in 1539. Garrido was essentially out of work. Here was a man who had helped topple one of the world's richest empires, and just sixteen years later he found himself poor and increasingly forgotten.

It was doubtlessly in response to this decline in his affairs that Garrido petitioned the King (the *probanza* of 1537) in the final years of his life, proclaiming his service to the Crown and seeking assistance. He died in the mid-1540s in his middle sixties, according to some, leaving a wife and three children.

The politically correct among us are generally baffled as to what to make of the life of Juan Garrido. On the one hand, he was a Black man who succeeded in the European world at a time when such was considered all but impossible. For that achievement he is admired. But on the other hand, he committed questionable, "Spanish" acts, such as attacking the Indians, taking their land, relieving them of their wealth and enslaving them, along with imported Africans. For some, a Black man—read "victim" from the modern perspective—should not have been engaged in such aggressive activities. This part of his life is therefore generally passed over in silence.

This curious perspective qualifies him uniquely as an African but nullifies him as a human being. In the broader view, however, there is a good deal to be learned from this man's life. Rather than attempting to transform the world as he found it or simply withdraw into seclusion, he accepted the rules and conditions of that age, made the most of things, and risked everything in his undertakings. These were the harsh realities of harsh times. Had he acted otherwise, his name would not be known to us today.

My own inclination is to accept the marks that he has left on his time purely for what they were and thereby free him from anachronistically biased judgments. Such an approach extends to him consideration as the man he obviously desired to be. By this measure he is worthy of our attention, indeed even our admiration.

The Grumman Goose landing in the St. Thomas harbor.

CHAPTER 9

ANTILLES AIRBOATS, CHARLIE, & THE GOOSE

A NYONE WHO LIVED on St. Croix in the 1960s and 1970s remembers Antilles Airboats and the "Goose." The Grumman Goose was a squat, ungainly looking aircraft that sat low in the water, giving one pause for thought before climbing aboard. On take-off it lurched dramatically through the water of Christiansted harbor and droned loudly as it lumbered into the air. But what a sight it was as it banked to the west while crossing above the reef and then roaring off over the sea to St. Thomas! It was impossible not to hear its straining engines and follow it with the eye it until it became a tiny speck on the horizon. From its inception in 1964 until its demise after Hurricane Hugo in 1989, Antilles Airboats was an island institution, in many ways the salient symbol of the modern development of the Virgin Islands.

For many years the difficulties of inter-island travel impeded the islands' growth. From colonial times until well into the 19th century, sailing vessels laboriously plied the waters between the islands. In the 1930s, air travel made its appearance, but prohibitive cost, the inconveniences of airport-to-airport connections, and scheduling limitations all restricted the free flow of travelers. In 1964, Charles Blair and his Antilles Airboats changed all that and in the process left an enduring mark on our islands.

Charlie, as everyone called him, arrived in the islands with outstanding credentials. He was born on July 9, 1909, in Buffalo, New York, and as a young man learned to fly in San Diego. After a degree in engineering from the University of Vermont in 1931, he entered the Naval Air

Service for a brief stint. From 1933 to the outbreak of World War Two, he flew as a pilot for United Airlines.

During the War, he served in NATS (Naval Air Transport) and the ATC (Air Transport Command), testing and flying seaplanes in the North Atlantic. It was during that period that Charlie clocked some of the fastest Trans-Atlantic flights on record for that time. It soon became apparent that he was obviously a pilot a cut well above all the others.

After the War, he remained in Trans-Atlantic air transport, and in 1950, he became a pilot for the legendary Pan American World Airways. There he remained until his retirement in 1969 at the age of sixty. During that span, he made a number of other contributions to aeronautics and general aviation.

A foremost achievement in his flying career occurred in 1951, when he flew his P-51 Mustang named Excalibur III from New York to London in just over ten hours, a record for piston engines that stands to this day. That same year he piloted the same aircraft over the North Pole from Norway to Alaska in the world's first trans-polar flight, blazing a trail for subsequent commercial, over the pole flights. In 1959, he duplicated these flights over the North Pole in an F-100 jet aircraft. These feats earned him recognition as one of the world's foremost aviators.

During his years at Pan Am, Charlie continued to serve the nation in a number of capacities. He remained a Brigadier General in the Air Force Reserve, earning the Distinguished Flying Cross and the Harmon International Aviation Award. He also served in the newly formed National Aeronautics and Space Administration (NASA). In 1970, he capped off his illustrious career with an account of his exploits in his book *Red Ball in the Sky*.

Charlie came to the Virgin Islands in 1964. Those were the years of the Paiewonsky government when the Territory was poised on the verge of real economic development. On St. Croix, Hess Oil and Harvey Aluminum were just beginning to get started, creating thousands of jobs in the process and attracting immigrants from all points in the Caribbean.

ANTILLES AIRBOATS, CHARLIE, & THE GOOSE

The College of the Virgin Islands soon opened its doors and likewise brought in new people. At the same time, tourism flourished in St. Thomas, especially after the Cuban Revolution under Fidel Castro and the worst excesses of the Haitian dictatorship under François Duvalier in the late 1950s flattened tourism in those islands. St. Thomians were quick to take advantage of these new opportunities. Things were beginning to move in the Virgin Islands.

Enter Charlie Blair. In 1964, he decided that the time was right for a seaplane connection between the major islands of the Virgins, and he put his money where his mouth was. With a single Grumman Goose aircraft that he had purchased earlier from Naval surplus, he established the headquarters of Antilles Airboats in Christiansted, St. Croix. In those early years its base was located at the seaward end of the Pan Am Pavilion, where it roared landward up a ramp and discharged its passengers right in front of Sir Aubrey's famed Pig's Ear Bar and Restaurant.

Charlie headed the operation as its president but still found time to pilot flights between the islands. The genius of this modest beginning was in the direct connection between downtown Christiansted to downtown St. Thomas, offering frequent, short duration flights, with a tad of adventure thrown in at no extra cost. For many, it became like catching a cab between the islands, and, as such, it caught on fast. More importantly, it changed the way people and organizations did business.

The success of Antilles Airboats can be measured in terms of its rapid growth. By 1977, the fleet had grown to 23 aircraft, including 19 "Gooses," 2 Grumman Mallards and 2 large Sandringham's. With this expansion, the base of the operation moved to a new, larger area located at Watergut, further to the west along the beach of the Christiansted harbor, where offices, a cargo department, a maintenance shop, and a small restaurant sprang into being.

In a short time, the "Goose" assumed an important place in island society. Government workers and officials, teachers, private business people, and everyday folk all passed through that way-station, stopping in their passage to share conversations and a bit of "mellay" over a quick cup of coffee and a donut, filling the air with Spanish, English, Crucian, Papiamento, French Creole, and scores of other Caribbean dialects. It was in the transit area of the Goose that one could see how clearly multicultural our society had become and, really, how well we somehow all got on in spite of our differences.

Charlie made a fine life for himself in St. Croix. In 1968, he married the stunning Irish actress Maureen O'Hara, whose beauty had graced the screen in films such as "The Quiet Man," "Miracle on 34th Street," "The Hunchback of Notre Dame," and many others. Together they established a home on a hill overlooking Christiansted, from where Charlie could keep an eye on his Goose flock, taking off and landing. Charlie and Maureen made a striking pair as they made their way through town, mingled at the Airboats or had an afternoon drink with friends at the Café de Paris in King's Alley. They set the island abuzz when they were paid visits by Hollywood film stars such as John Wayne. There can be no doubt that they added a certain panache to the island and to the town.

Maureen O'Hara and Charles Blair, owners of Antilles Airboats.

On September 2, 1978, it all came to an end for Charlie almost as quickly as it had begun. Shortly before the landing of a flight to St. Thomas that day, the Goose that he was piloting developed engine trouble and plummeted into the sea. Charlie died on impact and went to the bottom with his seaplane. Most people, when they heard the news, simply could not believe their ears. No, not Charlie, the invincible aviator,

ANTILLES AIRBOATS, CHARLIE, & THE GOOSE

the master of the skies. But his time had come. He was buried with full military honors at Arlington National Cemetery in Washington, D.C.

Antilles Airboats continued on for another decade, for a time under the guidance of Maureen, providing an indispensable service to the people of the Virgin Islands. The final bell tolled, however, in September of 1989, when Hurricane Hugo raged through these islands, destroying everything in its path, including many of the aircraft of the "world's largest seaplane airline." Antilles Airboats effectively died on that day, but seaplane travel, established and developed by Charles Blair, has continued to this day as an integral part of island life.

Of the many things that I associate with life in St. Croix in the 1960s and 1970s before the onslaught of full development and relentless change was the prospect of an Airboat ride to St. Thomas on the Goose, sometimes even sitting alongside the pilot in the cockpit. Along with the midday languor of Jeltup's Bookstore, the energy of the Town Wheel restaurant, the informal elegance of the Club Comanche, the chatter of the Saturday market in town, the charm of the little old ladies, all seemingly named Miss Mary, who sold candy on the street corners under the galleries, along with the relentless siren that blasted the arrival of noon every day and the broods of chickens that picked their way slowly through the quiet streets, the Goose, with the roar of its engines and the mad hustle and dash of its departures, undeniably set the pace and tone of life in that time and imbued our little town with a character that those who knew it remember as both unique and unforgettable.

The UVI campus on St. Thomas.

CHAPTER 10

THE UNIVERSITY OF THE VIRGIN ISLANDS: OUR PROUD POSSESSION

OVER THE PAST forty-seven years the University of the Virgin Islands has made itself one of the preeminent social institutions in the Territory. It has produced thousands of graduates, sent hundreds on to professional and graduate schools, and launched the careers of scores of doctors, lawyers, and business people, to say nothing of a multitude of teachers. It has additionally provided a home for artists, writers, and creative minds from all parts of the world. It has fostered drama and musical culture in a number of diverse genres in several forums and venues. But it has not always been a stroll down the garden path. And it's this counter-distinction that has made its history a fascinating one.

Prior to 1917 during the Danish period, it was all but impossible for a Danish West Indian to study at a university in Denmark. During the American period, especially before the early 1960s, higher education remained a scarce commodity in these islands. Those with such aspirations who made it through high school had to travel either to Puerto Rico or to the Mainland United States to enter a college or university. Most of those few who did so, found themselves at Inter-American University in Puerto Rico or at Morgan State or Howard University stateside. The cost of travel, the harsh contrast in climate, and racial discrimination all lent a certain degree of difficulty to the endeavor.

In the late 1950s, attitudes toward higher education for Virgin Islanders on a local scale began to emerge. This was due in large measure to rapid economic development and to the growth of the need for more schools and teachers in the Territory. In the late 1950s, Frederiksted-born Governor John Merwin was the first to approach the idea of a college in the Virgin Islands. That lead was soon followed up by Ralph Paiewonsky (1907–1991), who was appointed Governor by President John F. Kennedy in 1961, where he served until 1969. In tireless pursuit of that goal, Paiewonsky appointed the Virgin Islands College Commission in 1960, and in July 1961, he hosted the Governors' Conference on Higher Education. The Governor's efforts bore fruit on March 16, 1962, when the Fourth Legislature of the Virgin Islands passed Act 862 that established the College of the Virgin Islands (CVI). Ralph Paiewonsky dedicated himself completely to the College's growth and well-being as Chair of the Board of Directors from that time until his death in 1991.

The College of the Virgin Islands first opened its doors on St. Thomas, in July 1963, on a 175-acre tract of land provided by the federal government. The following year, 1964, a second campus opened on St. Croix at Estate Golden Grove on 130 acres. From the onset, the St. Croix campus was envisioned as a "feeder campus" to the main center in St. Thomas, an arrangement that occasioned some discontent and rivalry in the years that followed.

The St. Thomas campus sits perched on a hillside overlooking several of the incomparable beaches and bays on the island's south shore. It began modestly enough from two U.S. Marine Corps barracks structures and grew steadily from those modest beginnings. The St. Croix campus, on the other hand, took shape around a plantation building on Estate Golden Grove at mid-island and its adjacent structures that had been a central part of VICORP. Previous to that, the land and its estate structures had served as the residence of merchant and planter A. J. Blackwood, who owned and supervised from that modest hillock some of the island's most important estates at mid-island.

The first Board of Trustees, appointed in 1963, named Dr. Lawrence C. Wanlass to serve as the College's first president, and he proved admirably well-suited to the task of developing the campus, its programs, and its curriculum. At the beginning, the College offered only two-year associate degrees, but in 1967 it ventured its initial BA degree programs in Liberal Arts and Education, producing its first graduates in 1970. In 1976, the first MA degrees were conferred in Education. The young institution was quickly on its way.

In those early years it was nothing less than a delight to witness the eagerness with which our Crucian people embraced the fledgling institution, sacrificing their afternoons and evenings to books and learning. In one class I was fortunate enough to have as students the likes of Jada Mae Sheen, Kenneth Mapp, William Cissel, and Camille Macedon to name only a few. From my perspective, the story of CVI/UVI can best be written in terms of what folks such as these took from our university and then subsequently gave back a thousand-fold to our community.

Over its forty-seven-year history, UVI has been served by five presidents, namely: Lawrence C. Wanlass (1963–1980); Arthur Richards (1980 1990); Dr. Orville Kean (1990–2002); Dr. LaVerne Ragster (2002–2009); and most recently Dr. David Hall (2009–).

Under the Wanlass presidency (1963–1980), the College of the Virgin Islands took a number of important developmental steps forward, offering new degree programs and expanding the curriculum. The Caribbean Research Institute was created, opening the way for research by college and area scholars. In 1972, CVI received land grant status from which followed the establishment of the Cooperative Extension Service (CES) and the Agricultural Extension Station (AES). These two new departments enabled the college and its faculty to make a solid impact on community affairs.

The Wanlass presidency was fruitful in other ways as well. The Ralph Paiewonsky Library was established at the very onset and grew into one of the finest research libraries in the region. The Reichhold Center followed soon after, providing the College and the larger Virgin Islands community with access to theatre and to a wide array of performing arts. The St. Croix campus, which had been limited to Golden Grove plantation structures and to some of the limited facilities of the defunct

VICORP undertaking for over a decade, took a big step forward with the opening in 1976 of the Melvin Evans Center, which housed administrative offices, classrooms, a theatre, a bookstore and the library, and it remains the nucleus of the campus to this day.

Dr. Arthur Richards, former Virgin Islands Commissioner of Education, was inaugurated as second president in 1980. Under his direction, the College of the Virgin Islands became the University of the Virgin Islands on October 14, 1986, a move that has paid rich dividends in terms of attracting academic recognition and competent faculty. In that same period, UVI was named to the national roster of American HBCUs, (Historically Black Colleges and Universities). And not least, the Board of Trustees approved the creation of a Research and Technology Park, which, unfortunately, has been slow in getting off the mark.

For its third president, UVI reached into its own faculty ranks and selected in 1990 Dr. Orville Kean, professor of Mathematics. Under his leadership, the St. Croix Campus made a number of important advances. In general, the campus expanded, adding the Nursing Complex and the important Ralph D. DeChabert Virgin Islands and Caribbean Collection to the library. In addition, dormitories, a dining hall, an auditorium, and a student center were added. Dr. Kean also oversaw the establishment of the Eastern Caribbean Center, The William MacLean Marine Science Center, the Sports and Fitness Center, the daunting task of curriculum and organizational reform, and the gradual outreach of UVI to other islands in the Caribbean.

Those years, however, were not without their difficulties. In 1989 and 1995 respectively, Hurricanes Hugo and Marilyn slammed the two campuses exceptionally hard, forcing closure and the shutdown of instruction for the first time in the institution's history. In the face of those hardships, the UVI community reacted in concert, with administrators, professors, staff, and students alike all pitching in with their labor and high spirits in the effort to bring the university back on line. Those who lived through those times experienced a sense of harmony and fellowship that bound them firmly together for many years into the future.

THE UNIVERSITY OF THE VIRGIN ISLANDS

Dr. Laverne Ragster, a Professor of Biological Science at UVI, became the University's fourth president in 2002. She continued the reform work initiated by Dr. Kean and also undertook several construction projects on the St. Croix campus, namely the Northwest wing for much-needed faculty offices, the renovation of the former Golden Grove plantation house, and the building of the Great Hall, used primarily as a meeting area.

Dr. David Hall, former Professor of Law and Dean of the Law School at Northeastern University, assumed the UVI presidency in August of 2009. Although it is too early to envision where the next five years will carry UVI and Dr. Hall, he has shown himself to be an attentive listener and a fast learner. He has vowed to place emphasis on shared governance and improving student retention and graduation rates. He has also pledged to work closely with the V.I. Department of Education to improve overall education in the Territory.

In spite of all the development and progress, UVI has not been without its fair share of problems over the past nearly five decades. From the onset, some Crucians felt that the table was tilted too heavily in favor of St. Thomas. That discontent led to the creation of the posts of Chancellor and Provost, located at times on the St. Croix campus. But it remains a well-established truth that the tail never wags the dog, as some characterize the inter-island relationship. Academically speaking, there has been a long concern over the matter of academic standards, attrition rates, and the predominance of remedial programs required by many incoming students. These problems are chronic and endemic and have proven quite resistant to productive change in large part because they are passed along through the Territorial public education system.

Some problems are of a cultural and societal nature and therefore run even deeper. Parallel to a similar phenomenon in the States, female students have come to dominate in all areas of university activity, greatly outnumbering males, in some areas by as much as a 70 to 30 ratio. Similarly, for many years, native-born Virgin Islands students have found themselves in a pronounced minority in relation to students from other

SEA GRAPES AND KENNIPS

The palm-way entrance to the UVI campus on St. Croix.

parts of the Caribbean. These are developments that few expected when the College opened its doors in the early 1960s.

Perhaps because of this latter relationship, the university has experienced mixed results in the matter of self-identity and self-definition. Does the university have its own culture, its own set of standards, and clearly defined values, in the manner as does the University of the West Indies, for example? Many would respond in the negative to this question, pointing to the open door admissions policies, the remedial programs, and the high attrition rates by a highly mobile student population as probable causes. These matters will have to be addressed in the very near future if UVI is to move on to the next level of academic performance.

However all this may be, there remains a clearly positive side to the story. UVI has served a population that may have otherwise found a college education completely beyond its reach. But indeed, thousands among them have passed through the university's portals, going on to fill important ranks in our island society, graduates such as Alphonso Andrews, Yvette de la Banque, Magda Finch, Simon B. Jones-Hendrickson, Jennifer Nugent-Hill, and Marvin Pickering to name but a few. Many have continued on to higher education on the U.S. mainland and elsewhere. How many schools of comparable size and such short lifespan can match UVI's two Rhodes Scholars, in the persons of Ian Quincy Quinlan and Richard Skerritt?

All things considered, UVI has proven to be a remarkable experiment in self-help and boot-strap development, one in which all Virgin Islanders can take a measure of pride and satisfaction. If the next fifty years turn out to be as challenging, enriching, and profitable as have been the last forty-seven, then UVI will have by far surpassed the dreams of its founders and of those who have since then labored so long and so diligently in the University vineyard.

Ward M. Canaday, 1885–1976, U.S. businessman and St. Croix farmer.

CHAPTER 11

WARD M. CANADAY: AMERICAN INDUSTRIALIST & CRUCIAN FARMER

USUALLY HISTORY is about remembering. But in some cases it has involved forgetting. Events can conspire to cause a person or an event to more or less disappear. It is the job of the historian to go back and fetch the forgotten and then bring it back and lay it before us, for better or for worse. Such is the story of Ward M. Canaday, who for more than thirty years exerted a strong influence on events in the Virgin Islands. Today, however, his name has been forgotten by all but a few Virgin Islanders.

In the early 1930s, the Virgin Islands were emerging from the Naval administration that had lasted from 1917. The islands at that time found themselves badly in need of economic development, meaningful direction, and sound identity. The situation had in fact become so dismal that President Herbert Hoover, after a visit to the islands, characterized them infamously as an "effective poorhouse."

The U.S. response to those conditions consisted of the setting up of a civilian administration and the creation of the Virgin Islands Company. The latter of these aimed at reviving sugar production on St. Croix and the establishment of tourism on St. Thomas. Not long after came the passage of the First Organic Act (1936) that created civilian government. It also encouraged the development of political parties and popular participation in island government. Virgin Islanders were in those years taking their first uncertain steps forward as World War Two broke out. It was into this milieu that Ward Canaday arrived.

SEA GRAPES AND KENNIPS

Ward Murphy Canaday was born on December 12, 1885, in New Castle, Indiana. He was from a family of modest means but managed to attend Harvard University. He then began his career in the kitchen cabinet industry in Indiana, where he introduced the idea of a payment plan in order to induce customers to purchase his product on installments. The idea was such a success that it soon spread to the automobile industry.

In 1916, he took a position as director of advertising for the Willys-Overland Company in the newly developing U.S. auto industry. He quickly made a name for himself there by setting up the first automobile credit company. From there he ascended through the company ranks over the next fifty years.

Like many other companies, Willys-Overland suffered severe economic losses in the depression of the early 1930s. Canaday played an important role in rescuing the company from bankruptcy. From there he rose to be Chairman of the Board (1936–46) and President of the Company (1950–63), establishing himself as one of the foremost business leaders in America and, at the same time, making a fortune for himself.

Canaday's most significant achievement in his career in the auto industry was the creation and mass production of the Willys MV, the rugged military vehicle that later became known simply as the "Jeep" during the war. When the conflict broke out, the government put out a call for a prototype in forty-nine days: only Willys-Overland and one other company answered the challenge. Canaday put together a team that responded successfully to the call. The company then went on to supply 640,000 of these "Jeeps" during the course of the war, a major contribution to the winning of the conflict. In effect, he took Henry Ford's idea of the assembly line to a completely new level.

At the onset of his brilliant business career, a chance visit brought Canaday to St. Croix in the 1930s. He was immediately attracted to the island, not just by its quiet charm but as well by what he considered its potential. Sugar had declined precipitously in the past decade and land—large tracts of it—were available at bargain prices. Canaday was

WARD M. CANADAY

unable to resist. At one stroke of the pen, he became in 1936 one of St. Croix's biggest landowners, acquiring Estate Annaly and a number of estates located around it. He envisioned an opportunity to make money for himself while at the same time using his expertise to develop a backward economy.

His idea was a simple one. The U.S. Government had recently made a commitment to assist the islands by setting up the Virgin Islands Company on the New Deal model to develop and promote the cultivation of sugarcane. The goal of Federal officials was to put Virgin Islanders to work as small landowners and cultivators of the soil, prosperous peasants if you will, who could pay their own way. Canaday felt that whatever government could do, private enterprise could do better, quicker, and more efficiently. And who in the private sector might do that better than Ward Canaday, a proven success in American business? The business and industrial leader therefore became a Crucian farmer.

By 1946, he had acquired more land, in all amounting to approximately 5,000 acres in the fertile north central section of the island, about 10 percent of all arable land on the island. It was a sound investment due to the advantages offered by the local tax structure. Canaday cleared land, did contour plowing and fertilized his fields in the hope of increasing his land's yield. The water table, however, was low and that limited production, at least initially. It was typical of the Canaday method to identify the problem and then devise a direct means to solve it. In this case, he built ponds and dams on his acreage with the result that the water table rose and production grew.

As time passed, it became increasingly evident that cane cultivation would not solve the island's economic problems. Canaday was among the first to turn to cattle raising. He imported eight fine bulls from the King Ranch in Texas, giving several of them to other farmers as an incentive and keeping the balance for himself. In a short time, his meager, original herd grew into over a thousand head, and meat production was underway. The present Annaly Farms is the result of that initial venture.

SEA GRAPES AND KENNIPS

Annaly Mill, the Canaday residence on St. Croix.

Ward Canaday was a people-person, and, clearly, this was one of the reasons behind his success in St. Croix. He made fast friendships with numbers of people and drew them into his confidence. It seemed to many that he remembered the names of everyone he ever met. One such friendship was with Ralph George, a Crucian native from Grove Place, who came to manage the Canaday household on St. Croix. Another was Frits Lawaetz, farmer, businessman, senator, and raconteur, known affectionately by locals as the "Bull of Annaly." Frits became the manager of Canaday's estate and business interests during his frequent absences; their long working relationship produced positive benefits for both men, as well as for the people of the island.

WARD M. CANADAY

Canaday's presence also had positive benefits for tourism. Over time, he and Lawaetz cut a road that ran along the ridgeline through the hills above his several estates. He was of the opinion that the great beauty of the island's northwest corner deserved to be seen and appreciated. That project became the present day Scenic Road. One day, he drove a visiting friend over that road, one Laurence Rockefeller, who commented that the lovely land down below would make a wonderful golf course. Some time later, the Fountain Valley Golf course, now Carambola, was built by Rockefeller on that very spot. Canaday had a knack for making things happen.

It is nothing short of amazing that Canaday became as involved as he did in local affairs, given the intensity of his business interests stateside. In the early 1940s, he promoted the idea of aluminum processing in the islands to provide a cost-saving shipping advantage. He worked with local politicians to use his influence in Washington to have the federal taxes collected in the Virgin Islands returned to the islands. And he was outspoken in his support of the political advancement of his adopted tropical home. He served on the board of directors of Virgin Islands Corporation (VICORP) and held the important position of co-chair on the Caribbean Commission (1948–52). In all of these activities, Canaday showed himself to be tireless in his energy, progressive in his thinking, and well ahead of his time.

The reputation for impressive accomplishments that he had developed during the War in high government circles he put into service for the Virgin Islands. He advised presidents Roosevelt, Truman, and Eisenhower, and they all sought and trusted his advice. In 1948, he managed to convince President Truman to visit St. Croix in the hope of promoting business development and tourism. The President passed an engaging afternoon at Canaday's splendid residence at Estate Annaly in the company of the scores of Crucians who were all Canaday's friends. The successful presidential visit was covered in all the stateside newspapers and put St. Croix's name before the nation for the first time.

SEA GRAPES AND KENNIPS

In 1964, Canaday sensed a sea change in the islands. A change in the tax laws threatened his ability to pass along his V.I. holdings to his family at his decease. And he was growing older. He therefore passed along nearly all his property to Bryn Mawr College and Harvard University, who sold them to the Rockerfellers, who in turn developed the property in the direction of tourism. Some of the land he directed to his faithful Frits Lawaetz, who created St. Croix's largest cattle and meat industry, which remains viable at the present. The legacy of Canaday's labors remains very much in evidence to this day.

Canaday was a self-made man who believed that one can advance as far as his talent and hard work will take him. Government, for him, worked best when it stepped aside and allowed private interests the freedom to get the job done. The federal government, he believed, would do best in the Virgin Islands if it allowed the locals to develop their own economy and thereby assert fiscal and financial independence from Washington's purse strings. Nearly all of his projects embodied the aim of showing both Virgin Islanders and Federal officials just how this might be accomplished.

Just as Canaday reaped rich rewards from his American experience, he also gave back to others in like coin. In the latter years of his life, he turned his attention increasingly to philanthropy and charity. He developed the Canaday Family Charitable Trust, from whence came numerous gifts and donations to worthy causes. The University of Toledo stood high on the list of such beneficiaries. Sizable grants went to Harvard University and Bryn Mawr College. The American School of Classical Studies in Athens, Greece, likewise benefited from Canaday's largesse. And in St. Croix, his name still stands proudly on the Library at the Good Hope School.

Ward Canaday passed from this life a short time after his 90th birthday, on February 27 of 1976. He lived a full, abundant life by any standard, expending every ounce of his God-given energy on formidable undertakings. He was variously a great success in business, an innovator in finance, a major contributor to his country in the wartime effort, a creator of a brand of auto (The Jeep) that still flourishes to this day, a farmer in the Caribbean, and a philanthropist and benefactor of various causes in his homeland. After all this, it is nothing short of amazing just how little is remembered here in St. Croix about this man who offered the island so much.

Wulff Joseph Wulff, 1809–1842, Danish official on the Gold Coast.

CHAPTER 12

AN AFRICAN TALE: WULFF JOSEPH WULFF, SARA MALM, & FREDERIK'S MINDE

BECAUSE WE LOOK BACK on history, we sometimes feel that past events are inevitable, predetermined, fixed in the manner that they turned out. That perspective can be illusory. All causes have unpredictable results, and all events produce consequences, most of which are unintended and unforeseen. In many ways a life can be likened to a path that constantly forks in its procession, and at every fork along the way there are choices and every choice has many possible consequences.

This state of affairs can be illustrated in the history of Denmark and her colonies. In the seventeenth century, the Danes decided to get into sugar production. That decision led to the acquisition of several islands in the Caribbean—the Danish West Indies. As a consequence of that move, it was judged that laborers from a similar tropical clime were necessary. The Danes therefore established trading stations and forts on the west coast of Africa—Frederiksborg (1659), Christiansborg (1661), Fredensborg (1736), Prinsensten (1784), Kongensten (1784), and Augustaborg (1787)—through which to procure slaves. It was these forts, by the way, that proved to be the connecting points between the people of the Gold Coast—Ashanti, Aquambo, Ga, and others—and the Danish Islands in the Caribbean—St. Croix, St. Thomas, and St. John.

Those military-commercial footholds along the Gold Coast required men from Denmark to serve them in various capacities—soldiers, sailors, traders, merchants, workers, and the like. The point is that this chain

SEA GRAPES AND KENNIPS

of causal events led to numerous curious encounters that no one could have predicted at the onset. This is the story of one such encounter and its curious consequences in the lives of two unsuspecting strangers.

This tale begins with the life of Wulff Joseph Wulff (1809–1842). He was born into a Jewish family in Randers, Denmark, on April 23, 1809. It was during his childhood that Jews in Denmark were given full citizenship rights under the Danish Monarchy for the first time. Wulff took advantage of that opening by becoming a lawyer; he hoped to enter administrative or governmental service. Residual prejudice and discrimination against Jews, however, remained a practical fact of life in Denmark, thereby imposing limits on the young Wulff's aspirations. He therefore looked abroad for opportunity.

Denmark, as mentioned above, operated a string of forts and lodges along the Gold Coast of Africa, present day Ghana. But those strongholds offered hard duty for those who served there, promising little more than a long, six-year contract, low pay, a severe tropical climate, exposure to harsh diseases, and the likelihood of an early death. Few were attracted to it. It was for those reasons that Wulff was able to land a position there.

Wulff arrived at Christiansborg near Accra in 1836, aboard the Danish vessel "Den Dansk Eeg." The arrival was greeted by the firing of cannons and the gathering of soldiers and men from the fort, all eager for news from Copenhagen. Since it was on average the general rule that only a single Danish ship or two arrived from Denmark along the coast per year, the disproportionate excitement that it caused gave the arriving young Dane an idea of the isolation that he was about to face.

He immediately took up his duties as *Surnummerrair* (Reserve Assistant) to the Commandant of the Fort. Though the transatlantic slave trade was officially ended by Denmark some thirty years previously, some trading in slaves did take place clandestinely, and slavery itself was still widely practiced along the Gold Coast and in most other parts of West Africa among Africans. Officially, the Danes were dedicated to trade, primarily in gold, ivory, and the production of palm wine oil.

WULFF JOSEPH WULFF, SARA MALM, & FREDERIK'S MINDE

It was to this business that Wulff had pledged himself to serve for the next six years.

However, the young newcomer had ambitious plans of his own that extended well beyond those limits. Soon after his arrival he met several wealthy merchants of European extraction, who worked independently of the official Danish establishment. These men built imposing residences, maintained stocked warehouses, and carried on extensive trade. Some became highly influential in the eyes of the young Wulff. One such merchant was Henrich Richter, who had property, business interests, and numerous slaves. Richter had also followed the local practice of taking an African woman as a quasi-wife, thereby taking care of his own domestic needs and at the same time creating ties with the local population. Wulff made no bones about accepting Richter as his role model.

In the beginning of his stay, Wulff greatly disliked nearly everything about Africa and his work there. He hated the heat, feared the diseases, found the food distasteful, and was often depressed with homesickness. One remedy for his estrangement, he was convinced, was to imbibe six bottles of Madeira wine per day! In his correspondence home, he swore that the practice was essential to his survival. Slowly, however, his sense of alienation began to change, when, in the course of his first year in Accra, Wulff met and took to wife Sara Malm, a so-called Mulatto from the Ga tribe.

Sara was a baptized Christian of mixed African-European parentage and had taken a European name to replace her African one, "Tim-Tam." Wulff found her attractive in many ways, and they soon entered a conjugal union, as was the custom of most Danish men on the Coast who found themselves isolated and alone during their service there. Although Wulff never called Sara his wife, but rather "his Mulatinde" (Mulatto), he treated her in every way as his legally married spouse. In quick succession she bore him two sons (Theodore Ulysses and Frants) and one daughter (Wilhelmina Josephina). In his letters to his family back home in Denmark, he revealed his respect for Sara, saying "she

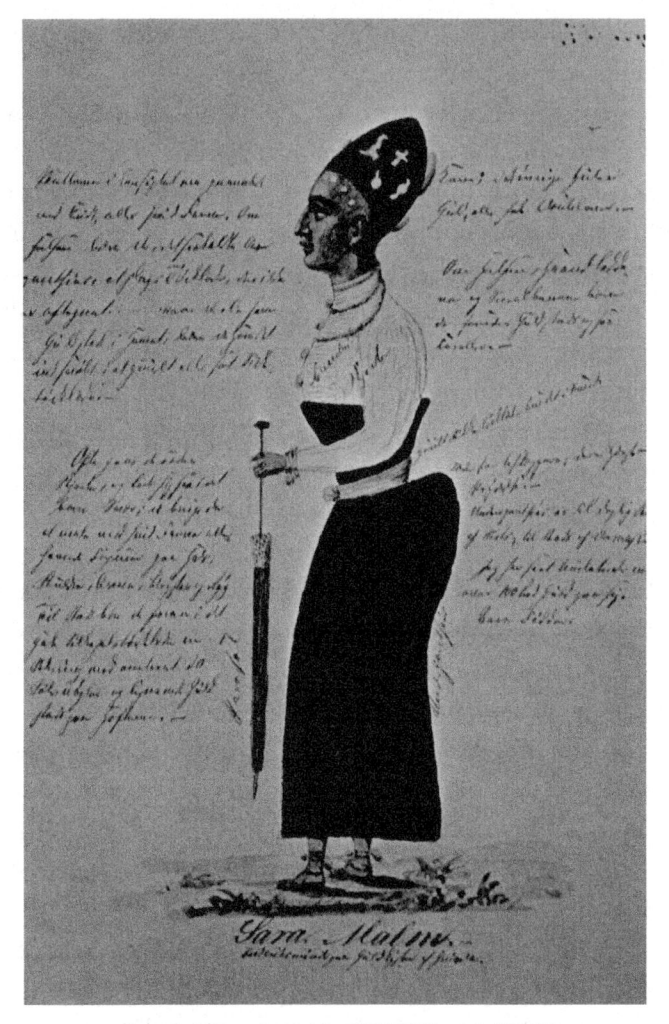

Sara Malm, the wife of Wulff Joseph Wulff.

could read, write and do arithmetic" and that she was perfectly able to oversee his personal affairs in his absence.

Wulff carried on a regular correspondence with relatives and friends in Denmark. In the beginning, there was a good deal of complaining in his letters. Gradually, however, he came to adapt to life in Africa in spite of the ever-present dangers. He came to like the food, he sired a family, adjusted to the heat, and started to learn the predominant Ga language from his wife. Most importantly, he began construction on a house, acquired slaves, and finally came to feel that he would never return to cold Denmark on a permanent basis. He even signed some of his letters back home to his family as "Your African."

During his first year, he and his family lived for a time in Fort Christiansborg, an uncomfortable arrangement to say the least. Wulff, however, had every intention of making Africa his home and he acted accordingly. He acquired a piece of property on the Castle Road in nearby Osu and in 1840 began to build a substantial house that he named "Frederik's Minde," for the Danish Monarch Frederik VI, who reigned from 1809 to 1839.

The outlay of capital involved in the undertaking would indicate that Wulff was already beginning to engage successfully in business on his own behalf. Such residences were few and far between, as well as expensive. Wulff, however, was smitten by the possibility of having his own residence, his "palace," as he sometimes called it. Even before the structure was completely finished, he moved his family in, and it was there that his children were born.

Wulff passionately looked forward to the end of his six years of service that he owed to the Danish Company. Clearly he hoped to carry on his own business as an independent individual and live in his beloved home with his family. But that was not to be. In December of 1842, just six weeks after the expiration of his contract, Wulff died of dysentery at Frederik's Minde in Osu. His family followed the African custom and buried him under his house, in this case in his basement. His daughter Wilhelmina Josephina was later buried at his side. Wulff was only thirty-three years old.

True to his own feelings, Wulff bequeathed his home and property, along with half of his financial wealth to his wife Sara Malm. The other half went to his family in Denmark. And true to their word, Sara and her children conserved and enhanced Wulff's beloved residence and preserved his memory. His name and family line have been particularly well cared for by his daughter Wilhelmina Josephina, who married a certain Major Cochrane, thereby passing on the Wulff-Cochrane name to hundreds of present-day Ghanaians, who are proud of their Danish forebear some eight generations after his demise. Through her, Frederik's Minde became a Danish-Ghanaian family house, whose traditions survive to this day. In 1894, the Wulff family in Denmark recognized Wulff's complete commitment to his African family and adopted homeland and sent his portrait there. It still hangs in Frederik's Minde to this day.

Wulff's life continues to have unexpected consequences. Fred Wulff, a young Ghanaian and distant descendent, recently had this to say about his Danish heritage. "[Black] Americans come to Ghana and proclaim proudly that they are 'coming home.' I too experience that same feeling when I come to Denmark. That was the fulfillment of a dream of many years for me to finally be able to see the land where Joseph Wulff came from."

In the short life of Wulff Joseph Wulff we witness a Dane embracing Africa, and Africa, in turn, embracing a Dane. This encounter raises an interesting question. Could it have happened in the reverse manner? Could an African under the influence of equally incomprehensible forces have made the same kind of transition to life in Denmark? In the next article, that question will be examined through the life of Frederik Pedersen Svane, a young African who, in the eighteenth century, made the long journey to Denmark and made a life there, far from Mother Africa.

The dwelling of Frederik Svane at Havrebjerg.

CHAPTER 13

A DANISH TALE: FREDERIK "AFRICANUS" SVANE & CATHERINE BADSCH

In another article, the life of the Dane Wulff Joseph Wulff in Africa was examined in some detail. The present article deals largely with the life of Frederik Svane, a mixed African-European who spent most of his life in Denmark. A comparison of the two life-trajectories provides an interesting commentary of the age.

The European presence on the so-called Gold Coast of West Africa in the seventeenth century began simply enough—the aim was to establish a few trading forts and get into the business of dealing in gold, ivory, and human cargoes. But what began as a simple idea soon grew complex. Treaties had to be signed with local chiefs and kings. Captives had to be obtained and sold as slaves. Trade goods had to be delivered across a long stretch of ocean. And not least, Danish workers were needed to serve in the forts.

Since few European women ventured out to the coast and since the European men who served there were tied to long contracts, several unintended consequences resulted very quickly from the colonial experience of the Danish men in West Africa. One such consequence was the tendency toward liaisons formed between European men and African women from several of the tribal kingdoms, producing offspring that were neither fully African nor fully European. The question then arose—what to do with this unexpected class of people?

The Europeans considered the Africans to be heathens, badly in need of religion and civil manners. The former were taking away natural resources and human cargoes and offered in return cheap trade goods and Christianity. The christianization of the native population, in addition to providing a putative spiritual benefit, was regarded as means of rendering the natives easier to deal with, more manageable, less hostile. So it was that the colonizers entered into a rudimentary form of missionary work.

It was soon discovered, however, that the undertaking was more complicated than first imagined. To read the Bible, take part in the liturgy, and become good proselytes required a certain degree of literacy on the part of the natives. But how was that to be achieved? One possible solution began as an experiment, involving the employment of the people of mixed blood whom they had already engendered. They might be used, it was reasoned, to train their fellow Africans in European ways. This simple idea produced some interesting results.

Jacobus Elias Johannes Capitein (1717–1747) was one of the first such Africans to be sent to Europe. He was taken to Holland by a Dutch trader, and there he attended the University of Leiden, receiving an excellent education. He became an ordained minister in the Dutch Reformed Church and ironically enough, he published a defense of slavery in Latin. He returned later in his life to Elmina on the coast, where he preached and taught from 1742 until his death in 1747.

Another was William of Amo from Axim, who was taken to Europe as a young child. There he grew up as a protégé of no less a person than the Princess of Brunswick. He obtained a doctorate from the University of Wittenberg. When the Princess died, William returned to Axim after thirty years in Europe, during which span he lived more or less as a recluse. So long had William been gone from Africa that he had forgotten his native language and was scarcely able to function in the local culture.

Yet another was Phillip Quaque of the Fante nation who was taken to England in 1761 by an Anglican missionary. There he was trained and eventually ordained as an Anglican minister before he returned to Cape Coast in 1766, where he remained until his death in 1816. He established

FREDERIK "AFRICANUS" SVANE & CATHERINE BADSCH

one of the first European schools in West Africa for mixed-race children and natives.

Just such an experiment was undertaken in Denmark in 1727, when King Frederik IV (reigned 1699–1730) ordered that two young men of mixed Ghanaian-Danish descent be brought from the Gold Coast to Denmark for training. The King and members of the government were interested to know just how Africans would adapt to Danish culture and training, and moreover, if that training could be employed in the education of children in Africa.

The first of these young men was Christian Jacob Protten, the son of a Danish soldier and a Ga mother. He was born in 1716 at Osu, near the fort at Christiansborg. Protten is of particular interest to Virgin Islanders because during his subsequent stay in Denmark, he met and married a woman from St. Croix, a certain Rebekka Freundlich, who was active in the Moravian mission movement in the Danish islands. Protten did not adapt well to Danish culture and ways and quickly ended up back in Africa, where he lived out a conflicted career.

Frederik Svane was the second of the two young men at the center of the royal plan. Svane was born in 1710, also in the village of Osu, the son of a Danish soldier, one Hendrik Petersen, and a young African woman, who hailed from Teshi, a nearby village. At the age of ten, Frederik became a boy soldier as well as a schoolboy at the fort. After his father died, Frederik was taken in by the Danish Lutheran minister at the fort, a certain Elias Svane. The pastor took the young man to Denmark with him, where King Frederik IV developed an interest in him and stood as his godfather at his re-christening. At that same time, Pastor Svane adopted Frederik as his son and gave him his name.

After the baptism and sponsorship by the King, both Frederik and Christian Protten were sent to Sorterup near Slagelse for private tutoring by Pastor Svane. Both of them were off to a good start. When they advanced to the University of Copenhagen, however, they both experienced difficulty in adapting. Protten returned to Africa in 1736, where he taught in several schools and eventually created a writing system for the Ga language. Svane struggled on with his studies in theology in Denmark for a time.

In 1734, the now Frederik Svane married Catherine Marine Badsch, a young Danish woman. Interracial marriage was altogether rare at that point in Danish History, and the couple must have paid a dear price for their venture. More than likely, the unfavorable attention that they attracted was the reason why Svane left the University and departed for Africa with his new wife the following year. This was a bold move indeed for a man with such limited means.

After his return to the Gold Coast, Svane worked at Christiansborg as a clerk and teacher and was involved in the slave trade with the Danish West Indies. During that same time, Catherine became pregnant and bore Frederik a son, named Johann Frederik. During her pregnancy, she was so harassed by the Danish officials and soldiers in and around Christiansborg that she soon thereafter returned to Denmark with their son. She found refuge in the home of Frederik's adopted father, Pastor Svane.

In the meantime, Frederik, still on the Gold Coast, drifted into trouble. He lived with an African woman and became known as an adulterer. Worse, he became involved in petty intrigues and disputes at the fort, activities that landed him briefly in prison. These events he recorded, from his own perspective, of course, in a memoir entitled *The General Description*.

In time, Frederik came to regret his circumstances and petitioned to be allowed to return to Denmark to join his wife and child. When he was granted that permission, he sailed to Denmark and attempted to restart the Danish part of his life. He obtained a position as parish clerk and teacher in Havrebjerg, one of the estates of the well-known Ludvig von Holberg (1684–1754), who is widely recognized as the greatest writer in the history of Danish literature. There he served from around 1749 until 1785.

During that stretch, Frederik continued to experience personal difficulties. In succession, he suffered a falling out with the notoriously par-

FREDERIK "AFRICANUS" SVANE & CATHERINE BADSCH

*Ludwig Holberg, 1684–1754,
Denmark's greatest literary figure
and employer of Frederik Svane.*

simonious Holberg in a dispute over wages. Then he quarreled repeatedly with Joachim Gynther, the parish pastor on the estate, over various rather minor matters. In the end, he was censored by the bishop. So his time there was generally not a happy one.

In his later years, Frederik was afflicted with blindness. His condition forced him to leave his position as parish clerk, whereupon he and Catherine took up residence in a small dwelling near the Havrebjerg mill. One year later a fire forced them out of that dwelling. With no income, no place to go, and sickness and old age upon him, Frederik was at the end of the line. Catherine left him to go live with her son and his wife in nearby Gudum, whereas Frederik was admitted into the hospital at Slagelse as a pauper.

Frederik's troubled journey came to an end in 1789 when he died blind, without resources, and in poverty. His wife Catherine passed in the following year. What became of his son is not known. Svane was buried in an unmarked grave in Slagelse in Sjælland. He left little behind him to mark his memory beyond his name carved in Latin on the desk of the parish clerk at Havrebjerg: "Fridericus Petri Svane Africanus," thereby marking the African, Danish, and academic aspects of his life journey.

Frederik Svane and the previously studied Wulff Joseph Wullf shared a number of parallels in their lives. Both left their native lands for foreign climes at a young age. Both adapted relatively well to their new homes. Both entered into interracial marriages long before such unions were recognized as even marginally acceptable. Both men died in their adoptive lands. But the similarities end there.

Wulff died young but amassed some wealth, engendered a large family, and has been well remembered to this day in his adopted Ghana, whereas Svane lived into old age at seventy-nine but died in poverty, left only one known son, and has been largely forgotten by posterity in Denmark. The experiment would tend to argue that Ghana at that time was a good deal more welcoming of outsiders than was Denmark. In the final analysis it can be said that both men, with their similarities and their differences, were living witnesses to the great colonial collision between continents, countries, cultures, and peoples that so characterized their time and so deeply affected so many lives.

The eye of a Cape Verde hurricane over the Caribbean.

CHAPTER 14

VISITORS FROM THE SEA: CAPE VERDE HURRICANES

MAN PROPOSES and God disposes, according to the ancient wisdom. Although we humans are a part of the divine plan here on Earth, we would prefer to think we should have our own way in things. The creator, however, has seen fit to grant us life and opportunity but only in the face of multiple perils. Indeed, what appears to be a peaceful blue planet floating easily through space is in reality a conflicted sphere torn by deadly but altogether natural, internal forces—earthquakes, volcanic eruptions, tidal waves, glaciers, plagues, tornadoes, and hurricanes. Of these menaces to the human plan of order and regularity, it is the hurricane that poses the greatest threat to human life here in the Caribbean.

From July through October, we speak little about the windy monsters, but they constantly occupy our attention. Such has probably been true since the first of our species set foot on these islands some 5,000 years ago and saw the great storms as the manifestation of the presence of an angry god—Juracán, about whom they spoke in tones of awe. But it is now December and the season of storms has once again passed. Perhaps we might venture a few words about them—in a low voice, of course.

In the course of his four voyages to the Caribbean, Christopher Columbus was the first European to experience severe storms, which today would be called hurricanes. He learned quickly that if the rewards of the Caribbean were potentially great, the dangers of pursuing them in those waters were equally great. But what was the nature of these storms and where did they come from?

SEA GRAPES AND KENNIPS

Let us imagine that we are in a satellite above the Earth looking down from space at the central Atlantic Ocean. The life cycle of a Caribbean hurricane is played out in that vast swath of the Earth that stretches from southern Sudan in East Africa all the way to Central America, the East coast of North America, and the open seas of the North Atlantic.

The forces that give rise to such a storm, feed its development, and guide its path over several thousand miles are many and complex. But they can be summarized as the following: accruing solar radiation; rising ocean temperatures; prevailing westerly winds and air movement; heat differentials and thermal transfers; the rotation of the earth; and the cyclonic movement of air masses. These elements come together in the following manner.

As the sun approaches the summer solstice in the northern hemisphere, its rays strike the ocean surface more directly. Less sunlight is therefore reflected and more of it is absorbed directly into the ocean's waters. Toward the middle of summer those waters are heated to their maximum temperatures. When they reach 80 degrees to a depth of 160 feet, sea water is capable of spawning and nurturing large storms.

At the same time, the sands of the Sahara desert are being similarly heated. As rain falls in east Africa, it moistens the air, which moves westward across the vast expanse of super-heated sands on the prevailing winds. By the time these humid air masses reach the west African coast and move out over the coastal Atlantic waters, they begin to form storm cells and to increase in wind velocity in the area just south of the Cape Verde Islands, hence the name. In essence, this process is nothing more than the natural transfer of heat from one medium to another. What we now see from our orbital perch is the formation of cloud masses moving westward in what appears to be disorganized confusion.

What occurs next is the appearance of a line of storms, a wave, so to speak, of rain cells, characterized by lightning, thunder, and rain. Under the force of the regular rotation of the Earth on its axis, the heated, moisture laden mass of air in the linear wave begins a slight rotation in a counter-clockwise direction in the same manner as do all airborne

VISITORS FROM THE SEA: CAPE VERDE HURRICANES

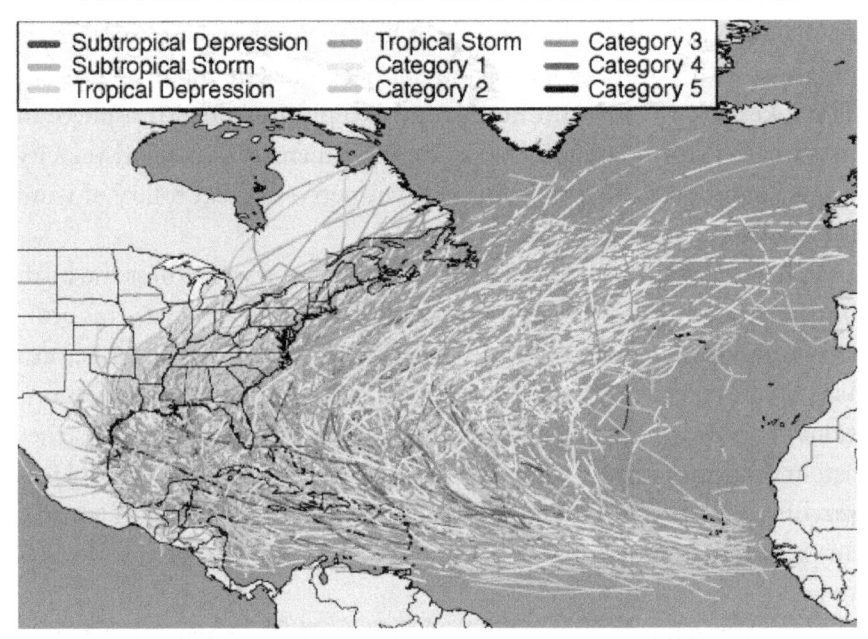

Hurricane tracks showing typical paths of storms crossing the Caribbean and the Gulf.

trajectories in the northern hemisphere—under the Coriolis effect. This dynamic weather system at this point assumes several varieties of movement. First, the entire mass moves slowly forward in a westerly direction. Secondly, it begins to rotate in a counterclockwise direction. And thirdly, air at the ocean's surface, absorbing heat from the water, begins to rise, carrying moisture upward with it.

But what are the forces that transform this natural, local process into a true hurricane of awesome proportions? Scientists are not yet altogether certain. In part, the answer might lie in the interplay of pure chance. Single cells often remain just that, moving in an unorganized manner, dropping rain and then petering out. Those that grow into troughs, depressions, tropical storms, and eventually hurricanes might well be the result of a number of these cells merging together, lending their combined energy to a greater entity in a critical transformation.

The nascent storm now has a vast stretch of warm open ocean before it, on which to feed. In the solitude of the sea, with no land to block its progress, with no upper level wind shear to prevent the formation of a "smokestack effect," with no disruptive high pressure atmosphere in its path, the storm strengthens, its rotation increases, its wind velocity grows, and it takes on a well-formed symmetry—a great rotary of wind moving about a distinct center, or eye.

When the wind speed reaches 74 miles per hour, we witness the birth of a hurricane, one of the most powerful forces on our planet. This ordinarily occurs somewhere in mid-Atlantic to the east of the Leeward Islands. From that point, a fledgling category one hurricane can continue to grow in size and strength in a matter of hours until it reaches astounding proportions, the most powerful among them capable of reaching speeds of 195 miles per hour. It is then bestowed with a name, an identity, and a persona. What matters most is where it now decides to go.

Cape Verde hurricanes generally follow one of four general east-west trajectories in their brief but ferocious life-spans. The first trajectory, or track, sees them entering Caribbean waters somewhere between Barbados and Dominica and passing across the Caribbean Sea just to the south of the Greater Antilles, turning north finally into Central America or the Gulf of Mexico. The second type track initially makes first land between Dominica and the Leeward Islands and moves directly over the islands of the northern Lesser Antilles, including the Virgin Islands, and the Greater Antilles, turning north toward Florida and the Carolinas. The third trajectory passes just to the north of the Caribbean Islands and then proceeds in a northwesterly arc toward the east coast of North America and Canada. And the fourth kind turns north prematurely and rages into the Central Atlantic, without colliding with a major land mass.

After all has been said about origins, the reality is that living in the Virgin Islands is a bit like being a bowling pin standing helplessly at the far end of a lane in a bowling alley. We know the ball is coming, but we just cannot quite figure out exactly which of us it's going to send reeling.

VISITORS FROM THE SEA: CAPE VERDE HURRICANES

So it has been over the years. Andrew and Gilbert passed to the south. Katrina passed to the north. Luis veered abruptly and headed off into a much-appreciated North Atlantic oblivion. But Hugo, well, everyone remembers Hugo, and nothing more need be said about that visit by the devil himself.

On September 19, 1989, I surveyed my broken home the morning after Hugo and had this to say:

> "I turn to face the house. What I see is a broken-toothed, blind-eyed hulk of a thing where I once ate and slept and played with my children. It takes me 30 minutes to find a way in. I must climb over ceiling beams, broken walls, glass, nails, twisted metal—it's all there, only re-arranged. Inside, water is pouring through what was once a roof as if the place had been bombed. The walls are broken or cracked along the bond beam. Everything has been smashed beyond recognition and left in the oddest postures. There is no way to enter our bedroom; a mass of debris blocks the doorway from floor to ceiling. The bedrooms of my children have simply collapsed. Half of my books have just disappeared into the air; those remaining litter the floors, twisted and soaked. My computers are either smashed or soaked. Personal files have been ripped apart. And personal items, especially photos, are scattered everywhere and ruined. Even our collective past in these precious few photos has not been spared. So it is throughout the house—a trail of utter destruction and desolation. I look at it all in disbelief. Angry, impotent words lodge in my throat. I cannot go on talking about it."

Cape Verde hurricanes subject everything they hit to great damage through their strong winds, tornadoes, strong rains, flooding, mud slides, and sea surge. The results can be devastating.

In addition to not knowing where hurricanes will strike, there is also the question of when. Our local "Hurricane season" stretches from July through October. Most years there are at least a dozen or so storms that pass through our region, perhaps three of them as category three and above in strength. With luck, in some years, the storms pass all around us, and we are spared their destructive force, as was the case this past year. In other times, we have suffered as many as three direct hits in a single year. There simply is no telling when they will hit because the matter is fraught with a number of indiscernible variables.

The first recorded hurricanes to strike the Virgin Islands occurred in the 1690s, hitting both St. Croix and St. Thomas. In 1726, three killer storms struck St. Thomas in the same season, the first time that such had occurred in living memory. In 1738, a powerful storm struck St. Croix, damaging the newly built fort in Christiansted. And from 1739 to 1751, the islands were inexplicably all spared such visitations. This dearth of storms is reminiscent of the period from the 1928 until 1989, during which time the Virgin Islands was spared any direct strike from a major storm.

From time to time, our islands have experienced monster storms that have left deep marks on our infrastructure, our lives, and our history due to their ferocity and destructive power. On August 31, 1772, St. Croix witnessed one of the great storms in her past, one that wrought great destruction and carried off many lives. That hurricane and the one that followed in 1785, according to Hans West, writing in 1793, "left traces of which are still seen in the ruins of collapsed walls and buildings."

In the 19th century, the Virgin Islands witnessed a number of memorable hurricanes, namely in 1827, 1837, and in 1867, the latter perhaps the greatest of all time. That same pattern of regular storms spaced across the century, punctuated by four to five great storms at longer intervals, continued through the 20th century. Just before the transfer of the Danish West Indies from Denmark to the U.S., the islands were hit hard in October of 1916. In 1928, the famous San Vicente Hurricane that so ravaged Puerto Rico also dealt a heavy blow to the Virgin Islands. And most recently Hugo, the most destructive hurricane in Virgin Islands history flattened St. Croix with a direct hit before rolling on to St. Thomas and Puerto Rico. Six years later, St. Thomas was leveled by her great hurricane, Marilyn. Who can doubt that future generations may well view the 1990s as perhaps the most perilous time in our long history?

VISITORS FROM THE SEA: CAPE VERDE HURRICANES

In the broad view of things we are forced to admit that what might be disastrous for humans and our societies is quite a normal phenomenon in nature. As a hurricane passes over the surface of the earth, it dissipates and transfers heat imbalances; it prunes older, weaker life forms in favor of the young and the strong; and it ends by settling the environment into a new balance and equilibrium. That is the science of it. The human response—the heartbreak, misery, and grief—is quite another thing.

Silk Cotton spirit tree.

CHAPTER 15

OBEAH, JUMBIES, AN' TING

FROM THE TIME of the arrival of the first Europeans to these islands, several Western religions have been introduced here—Lutheranism, Anglicanism, Moravianism, and Catholicism, these being the first among a number of others that came later. Within a short period of time, proselytizing of the newly introduced Africans was undertaken by these faiths with the aim of making them all Christians. But just beneath the surface of things, another powerful spiritual force was at work—Obeah from the African Motherland. While the vast majority of the enslaved did become Christians in one denomination or another—in many instances better ones than their European counterparts—the Obeah man and his system of spells persisted tenaciously, clinging on at the edges of society down to this day.

There are all kinds of theories about the origins of Obeah, some holding that it came from Ancient Egypt. Much more likely is that it stems from West Africa, in particular from what is today Ghana. It may be related to the Ashanti term, "Obayifo," meaning a "witch," or "vampire-like creature." It was carried from there to various islands in the Caribbean, especially those to which natives of the Gold Coast had been transported as slaves. Among these locations were Trinidad, Antigua, Jamaica, and, of course, the Virgin Islands. In those parts, Obeah took root and has persisted ever since.

Obeah beliefs were present in the Danish West Indies from earliest times. In outward appearance, the Obeah man was just another slave. Through training and apprenticeship, however, he had mastered a body of knowledge that rendered him powerful in the enslaved community and feared among the Europeans.

In essence, an Obeah man claimed to be able to harness the power inherent in the world and in nature for the purpose of directing it and using it in the casting of spells. Such spells might be positive in the sense that they might be directed to help an individual in matters of health, marriage, love, wealth, physical well-being, or simple luck. On the other hand, they might be negative in intent if they were aimed at bringing harm, loss, misfortune, or even death to an unsuspecting individual. Shamanistic practices such as these are nothing new or unique to the Caribbean and are widely known and practiced in other cultures around the world.

From this perspective, the Obeah man or Obeah woman was not a moralist teaching a spiritual code or offering salvation in the world to come. Indeed, when he provided a spell that was requested by a follower, he considered himself nothing more than a practitioner of his craft, for which he would receive respect and a recompense of one kind or another. The consequential responsibility for the effects of the spell lay with the person who had sought it out. And those consequences could be powerful and far-reaching.

In pursuit of his craft, the Obeah man possessed many talents and abilities. Above all, he was a first-rate herbalist. He had knowledge of and access to numerous plants and herbs, which endowed him with powers that ranged from healing to poisoning. He also understood human psychology and human social behavior. He was well acquainted with the strengths and weaknesses of the people whom he served. In a word, he was positioned to either serve life or destroy it. Most of the Obeah practitioners did both. In this regard, Obeah resembles Wicca, which arose in Celtic Europe centuries ago and still persists in several forms to this day.

An element of social control resulted from Obeah's powers. It was strongly believed, as one example, that the Obeah man could steal one's shadow, a poetic way of saying that he could capture and keep the soul of any individual. Some Obeah men carried around little boxes, or "caskets," as an ostentatious display of that very power. Needless to say, this practice forced his fellows to give him a wide berth in the slave community. This respect he could employ in order to control and direct social behavior.

Today, the practice of Obeah has a decidedly negative connotation. But it may not have always been that way. When the religion arrived from Africa it had both a positive and a negative side, the interplay of good and evil as in the case with most religions. The positive side that was practiced for the most part in the open was quickly sheared away by the European religions, especially by Moravianism, as a form of paganism. That left the negative side, the part that was pursued at night and in secret and that was able to escape the Western pressure and survive in secrecy, at least in part, down to this day. That was the dark side of Obeah.

Obeah men were able to convince many among the slave community that they were immune to death and punishment. By that belief they were able to embolden their fellows to resist the oppressive system that held them in bondage. As a result, slave revolts generally had an Obeah element, uniting the enslaved as one against the oppressor. On the other hand, it also exercised an extremely negative effect on the community, in that literally anyone could evoke its powers in the form of spells against anyone else.

Over a long period of time, suspicion among people came to be the rule of social relationships. When something went wrong, it could always be said that someone had "set" Obeah and the search for the culprit began, often culminating in retaliation, rightly or wrongly. Even today, Virgin Islanders are very cautious about relationships, wary, as one example, about "whom they will eat from." Overall then, Obeah has been, if anything, a source of disharmony among Caribbean people.

J. Antonio Jarvis, the noted Virgin Islands scholar and historian, wrote at length about this dark side of Obeah in the 1940s and took a very strong stand against it: "Most strangers are unaware of the dark currents of native life, and they never suspect the amount of fetishism, necromancy and plain poisoning that goes on under their upturned noses." Jarvis had the courage to say publically what many believed in private.

SEA GRAPES AND KENNIPS

Closely related to Obeah was a belief in spirits, locally called "Jumbies." This belief system is not unique or odd in world history—the Greeks had their Moirai; the Celts had their Faeries; the English, their Gremlins; the Germans, their Elves; the Irish, their Little People; the Arabs, their Jinn; the Danes, their Trolls, the Romans, their Penates, and others, their goblins and gnomes of one stripe or another. To this expansive group we can add our own Crucian Jumbies. Varieties of these assorted spirit beings have always been present in the development of the human spiritual consciousness, through which all cultures have had to pass on the way to an encounter with the singular divine.

Jumbies inhabit about every island in the Caribbean, sometimes having slightly different names and behaviors depending on the locale. They are related to but not identical with the Duppies of Jamaica and the Zombies of Haiti. As was the case with Obeah, they trace their origins to Western Africa. They are essentially malevolent spirits who cannot or will not find their way into the after world. When a person dies, so the belief goes, the soul from time to time does not readily make the transition to the other world but remains on earth as a wandering spirit or ghost. As such, these Earth-bound spirits become Jumbies, spreading fear, anxiety, and disharmony among humans as a result of their own unsettled state.

Crucian Jumbies can pop up about everywhere, but they particularly like to hang out in graveyards, deserted buildings, ancient trees, and generally dark, secluded places. Although they themselves are rarely ever seen, they can, according to their desire, take the shapes of different animals, especially dogs and cats, and even people from time to time. Often they are associated with strange sounds in the night. But usually they are best known by the things they do to trouble us—moving or hiding things, causing disruption or disharmony, and sowing deception and deceit. Among other nocturnal activities, they are particularly fond of bombarding a roof at night with stones.

They are equally known to take great pleasure in following people around at night and scaring the daylights out of them. You might, for example, "pick up" a Jumbie while passing through or near a graveyard after sunset, God forbid. No matter how fast you walk, the little devil will stick fast on your tail. To lose him, you might make a sharp turn, because Jumbies are prone to travel in straight lines. You might throw down some salt or rice grains, and the curious little chap will stop to count every grain, giving you time to make a break for it. Or when you go through a door, you might do so backwards, leaving your pursuer standing outside, not knowing how to follow you inside. Jumbies, the belief goes, are everywhere, and we simply have to learn to live with them.

Mocko Jumbies, now known largely as performers on festive occasions, once played an important part in all this. These elaborately costumed stilt-walkers also trace their origins to West Africa where they played a role in village life. Armed with a whip, hidden by a mask, and elevated above ordinary people in height, these long-legged fellows had the job of driving away evil spirits who took refuge in the village's sacred trees; it was necessary to expel the uninvited intruders before any sacred rituals could be performed. From that time to the present, however, their function, in particular here in the Virgin Islands, has changed considerably, now limited for the most part to colorful, high-level acrobatic dancing during celebrations and festive occasions.

Mocko Jumbies had all but died out by the 1950s, when they were fortuitously reintroduced into Virgin Islands culture by Willard John and Ali Paul. Today these daring acrobats are the delight of every tourist who sets foot on our island. So it is that while the Jumbies have had to remain underground, the Mocko Jumbies have enjoyed an entirely different destiny as public performers.

Obeah, Jumbies, and Mocko Jumbies all still occupy a place in the culture of the Virgin Islands today. But each of these in its own way has changed dramatically since it was introduced into these islands several hundred years ago. Whether we take delight in them or fear them, they have been and remain an important part of what makes these islands unique. At the same time, these modest insights might give us pause to consider where we have been on this long journey in order to readjust our sights on where we might now wish to go and on what we might prefer to leave behind.

Fritz Henle, 1910–1993, world-class photographer who resided on St. Croix during the second half of his life.

CHAPTER 16

FRITZ HENLE: ST. CROIX'S MASTER PHOTOGRAPHER

NUMEROUS PERSONS of international reputation have made their way to St. Croix over the years and even called this island home. William Hastie, a leading U.S. political figure, served as governor from 1946–1949. Ward Canaday, a U.S. industrialist and producer of the World War Two Jeep, established a farm on St. Croix in the 1930s and became deeply involved in local affairs until the 1960s. Victor Borge, the Danish pianist and entertainer, purchased a home in Christiansted and passed his leisure time there. Robert Oppenheimer, the father of the atomic bomb, came here in the 1950s and eventually settled on St. John. To this imposing list of notables should be added the name of the acclaimed German photographer Fritz Henle.

I first met Fritz Henle passing in the street in front of Jeltrup's Bookstore in Christiansted in the early 1960s. He was wearing his signature North Sea cap and red bandana around his neck and was attired in a neat khaki outfit. A large Rolleiflex camera was hanging from his neck. Speaking with him only briefly, I found him to be quiet, modest, and unassuming. I had no idea who he was or what he did. Later I came to know him rather well but always at a distance. In fact, in the early 1980s, I produced an hour-long television special on his life and work in the Caribbean for local television, but, unfortunately it was never shown. What follows might be regarded as a rather lame attempt to redeem that failure.

Fritz Henle was born in Dortmund, Germany, on June 9, 1909, the son of a well-known surgeon. Early in life, his father introduced him to the beauty of classical music. And he also loaned him his camera. Fritz fell in love with the music, but he married the camera. In the basement beneath his father's music room in the family home, he built a darkroom, and there he produced his first prints while listening to music drifting down from above. By 1928, at the age of nineteen, he had taught himself enough about photography to know that he wanted to spend his life as a photographer.

Shortly after 1930, he was accepted as a student at the *Bayerische Staatslehranstalt für Lichtbildwesen* in Schwabing, the artistic center of the city of München. There he was exposed to excellent teaching along with the influence of Modernism that was then prevalent in the German Weimar Republic. He graduated in 1931 and ventured out into the world equipped with the things that would enable him to become a world-class photographer, namely: a twin-lens Rolleiflex camera, a complete dedication to his profession, and a conviction that the world was filled with beautiful things. But nothing is simply a given in this life, and so the young Fritz entered into a long struggle for recognition and fame.

He first spent some time in Italy photographing Renaissance art for an academic project and was later sent by the publicity department of a large company to the Far East to do promotional work for the firm. From that experience came the first of his many books—one entitled *China* and another *Japan*. Both books did well and the photographer's career was launched.

Back in Germany during the 1930s and the rise of Nazism under Hitler, Henle found himself in an uncomfortable position. Although he was raised a Christian in his mother's tradition, there was a touch of Jewish blood on his father's side, a troubling matter in light of the rising tide of anti-semitism in Germany at that time. Henle sought to get out of the country amidst the uncertainty.

He had always longed to travel to the United States. In fact, he had studied English with an eye for realizing that very goal. In 1936, he made the leap across the Atlantic and quickly found himself swept up in the bustle of New York City. If it was a complex, impersonal metropolis, it was at the same time loaded with opportunity. Henle made the most of it and got into magazine photography by landing a job with prestigious *Life Magazine*. In 1938, that magazine sent the young photographer to Paris to do a photographic essay on the city and its inhabitants.

After three exhilarating weeks in Paris, Henle returned to New York with a portfolio of masterly work, perhaps his very best. Anyone who views it cannot help but be dazzled by the harmony of his compositions, the detail in his perspectives, the striking contrasts of his subjects with their ambient backdrops. In a word, he captured the soul of the city. These same traits would, to one degree or another, mark all of his subsequent work. They have to be seen in the fullness of their rich black and white textures to be properly appreciated.

Henle was stunned and disappointed when the editors at *Life* rejected his work. He would have to wait until 1944 when the Free French were reclaiming their city under Charles de Gaulle for the magazine to reconsider and publish the wonderful 1938 collection. With that stroke, Henle was on his way as a major magazine photographer in the American market. For the next several years his work appeared thereafter regularly in *Life, Saturday Evening Post, Harper's Bazaar, Town and Country,* and numerous other major publications.

During World War Two, he joined the Office of War Information and suspended his freelancing for a while to assist in the war effort. Until 1945, he traversed the country from end to end, making a detailed portrait of America and its people during the crucial 1940s. In this project, he worked alongside the likes of legendary photographers Jack Delano and Gordon Parks. It was during that stint, 1942, that he became a citizen of the American country that he had come to admire deeply.

After the war, Henle moved into fashion photography and quickly established a sterling reputation for himself in that new field. Fate was to soon intervene in his life. It was in 1947 after a cancelled fashion shoot in Venezuela that he accidentally visited St. Thomas in the Virgin Islands and was instantly enchanted by the natural beauty and charm of the islands. In the following year, he visited St. Croix and was immediately so charmed that he decided he wanted to live there. He

Photo of Christiansted harbor by Henle.

subsequently traveled to the island, completely smitten, as often as his schedule would allow. One editor of his remarked: "This [St. Croix] is an area about which Henle gets lyrical." His first photographic essay on the islands—*The Virgin Islands*—was published in a small book in 1949.

It was on St. Croix that he met and in 1954 married the beautiful Marguerite Schrader. Their union was an important event in his life, because it marked his commitment to make the island his permanent home. In quick succession they had three children—Maria, Tina, and Martin, all of whom eventually became photographers and artists in their father's footsteps as had been the case with Jan, another son by a previous marriage. In 1957, he built a home in Little Princesse overlooking Christiansted and its magnificent blue harbor, and the following year he sold his home and closed his studio in New York. He would call St. Croix home for the rest of his days.

FRITZ HENLE: ST. CROIX'S MASTER PHOTOGRAPHER

From his early years in the Virgin Islands in the 1950s resulted two important books, *Fritz Henle's Figure Studies*, a collection of stunning nude studies, and *The Caribbean*, a photo and text collection on the architecture, landscapes, and people of the entire Caribbean, including a number of perspectives of St. Croix. In his drive to capture what he considered the "beauty and truth of people and places," Fritz Henle continued to enjoy life and produce art prolifically.

Contract work for Alcoa Corp and Hess Oil enabled the photographer to travel broadly and continue his travel photography, as well as to explore the Caribbean. From these experiences came several more important books, including one on the art and technique of photography, which by that time had become quite a big fad in the United States. Additionally, from his close relationship with wealthy philanthropist Fairleigh Dickinson came two priceless works, *The American Virgin Islands: A Photographic Essay* (1973), a book without equal in Virgin Islands history and *Fritz Henle* (1973), a summary of the best work of his career in large portfolio. It was also during the 1970s that he met and photographed the famed Puerto Rican cellist Pablo Casals, resulting in 1975 in the publication of his acclaimed study of the great musician entitled simply *Casals*.

If Henle's first twenty years on St. Croix saw the production of the most mature work of his career then the last twenty years witnessed his dedication to exhibitions of that work, the collection of his prints, and the effort to make his work available to as wide an audience as possible. It was an impressive gift, fashioned in the tradition of Steiglitz and Eisenstaedt and offered in the manner of Adams, Weston and Dmitry. A broad selection of his works is available at the Maria Henle Studio at #55 Company Street, Christiansted (718-0372).

Fritz Henle remained active and completely engaged in his love of life and art until the end of his days. One suspects that when he passed from this life on January 31, 1993, his Rollei was not far from his side.

What is it that has made Henle's art so compelling for so long? Some critics have pointed correctly to the technical and methodological aspects of his work, that is, his abilities in the dark room, the attention he gave to printing, his concern for the quality of his working materials, his careful selection of expert collaborators, and, not least, his complete mastery of his camera. Others have taken note of certain more intangible qualities, such as his judicious eye for proper perspective, his obviously well thought out compositions, his clever use of subliminal contrast, and the studied detail that inhabits his frames.

Perhaps there was some other element as well. When I did the television shoot of Fritz in the 1980s, I interviewed him at length. One of his responses still stands out today. "What is required to become a good photographer," I asked him. "Don't take too many pictures," he responded. After looking at his work in detail, I came to understand, I think, what he meant by his cryptic remark. It is better to take one well-thought out picture rather than many mediocre ones, paying close attention to details, perspective, and composition. The analogy of a musician playing one beautiful note as opposed to many poor ones is unavoidable. Indeed, it is the spare harmony-in-composition aspect of Henle's artistic work, almost musical in its execution, that waits quietly there in the surface of the image for the eye of the observer to embrace it.

After his passing nearly twenty years ago, Fritz Henle still is saying to us: here is what I have seen and here is how I have seen it. There is beauty everywhere in this world and it is there to give delight to the eye, to ennoble the imagination, to impassion life to reach beyond the drab and the ordinary toward the ethereal. All you have to do is open your eyes and look. Fritz Henle once said, "One thing an artist can do in this world is to remind people that there is so much beauty that you only have to see it." Fitting words for an artist who was driven by the belief that beauty was everywhere.

A pirate attack in the open sea.

CHAPTER 17

BUCCANEERS, PRIVATEERS, & PIRATES

PIRACY, commerce, robbery, and trade all have some things in common: they involve a transaction between at least two parties that engages the primeval forces of supply and demand and the consequences of exchange. There is no scarcity of examples. The Vikings swept down over Europe in the eighth century and raided all the neighboring countries, leaving devastation in their train. So it has also been with the Barbary pirates, and their cousins in the waters of the Caribbean Sea and, more recently, in the South China Sea and in the Indian Ocean. But in addition to perpetuating acts of sheer theft, they stimulated trade and exchange and, ultimately, produced change.

In Caribbean history, sea roving has taken three forms: buccaneering, privateering, and piracy. These groups all shared certain behaviors, but at the same time each was distinct. The buccaneers trace their origins to the northern coasts of the island of Hispaniola in the late sixteenth century. Small groups of men who had run away from organized society formed associations that hunted and killed feral cattle (originally they were called "cow-killers"), dried the flesh over Taíno smokers called "boucans" (hence the name "boucaniers"), and then sold the product from their sailing canoes to passing ships as sea provisions. It was not long before these entrepreneurs found that it was even more profitable to rob their seafaring clients than to provision them. So they took to the sea and became seaborne robbers.

In 1625, those "buccaneers" set up an outlaw colony on the small island of Tortuga, which lies just off the north coast of present day Haiti. The Spaniards tried on several occasions to drive them out, but each time

SEA GRAPES AND KENNIPS

they returned and grew even stronger. Both English and French sailed as buccaneers from their small base there and for the most part attacked Spanish shipping and colonies in the western Caribbean. Over the course of the seventeenth century, they became known for their fierce hatred of Spaniards and for their ferocious, brutal behavior.

François L'Olonnais, a French buccaneer, was one of the most infamous and feared among these desperate men. In 1667, he and his cohorts sacked the cities of Maracaibo and Gibraltar in South America, torturing, killing, and raping hundreds of innocents, while making off with thousands of pieces of eight. Few escaped his wrath.

On one occasion, L'Olonnais captured two Spaniards from whom he desired information. When it wasn't readily given, he: "drew his cutlass, and with it cut open the breast of one of those poor Spaniards, and pulling out his heart with his sacrilegious hands, began to bite and gnaw it with his teeth, like a ravenous wolf, saying to the rest: I will serve you all alike, if you show me not another way."

L'Olonnais ravaged many an innocent before he died, just as he had lived. In his *History of the Buccaneers of America*, Alexandre Exquemelin tells us that the Frenchman was captured by natives at Darien, and they "tore him in pieces alive, throwing his body limb by limb into the fire and his ashes into the air; to the intent no trace nor memory might remain of such an infamous, inhuman creature."

The best known of all the buccaneers was Henry Morgan (1625–1688), a Welshman who landed in Jamaica as a young man and quickly became a freebooter. He sailed to the West Indies from Bristol as a bondman but quickly rose through the ranks as a sailor and captain at Jamaica during the ongoing conflict with Spain. Morgan led dozens of ships manned by hundreds of men in attacks on Spanish Main cities such as Porto Bello, Maracaibo, and Panama that netted him and his men hundreds of thousands of pieces of eight.

Morgan's success and excesses eventually earned him the enmity of the King of England, who stripped him of his position on the Jamaica Council and cut him adrift. He died in 1688 a broken man and was buried at the Palisadoes Cemetery, which sank into the earth four years later in an earthquake.

Privateering as a form of sea roving had very different origins. During the wars between the European nation states in the 16th and 17th centuries, navies had not yet been fully developed. Monarchs and admirals therefore often gave letters of marque, or specific commissions, to private individuals to attack certain enemy targets. These "commissioned officers," or "privateers" would then outfit a merchant ship with guns and a crew and head for the Caribbean. Whatever they captured, they might dispose of as "prizes" in special courts, keeping a share of the returns for themselves and for their crews. For a time, it worked rather well in the war that the northern European states waged against Spain.

Privateers also flourished during the American Revolutionary War and after the French Revolution, just as their British counterparts attacked Spanish shipping from the Battle of the Spanish Armada in 1588 until the eighteenth century. Richard Hawkins, Francis Drake, George Clifford, and Christopher Newton are names that figure prominently within their ranks.

As the wars of the seventeenth century drew to a close, most states turned against privateering and outlawed it because its leaders had become excessive and indiscriminate in the attacks. But as might be imagined, those "Brethren of the Coast" who were benefiting most from the practice were loath to give up their trade. After the end of the War of Spanish Succession, 1714, they came to be considered as simply pirates. Their actions were illegal and they were treated as mere criminals, punished by hanging if captured.

In spite of the dangers, thousands continued to be drawn into service under the black flag of the skull and cross-bones, some of them rising to levels of great infamy—Blackbeard, Captain Kidd, Tempest Rogers, and others. Their ships roved far and wide, from the Indian Ocean, through the Mediterranean Sea, across the Atlantic and into all parts of the Caribbean. Their targets of prey were merchant vessels whose cargoes they took for booty and whose crews and passengers they ransomed.

They needed ports where they might take their loot in order to convert it to hard species.

In the seventeenth century, St. Thomas, with its central location, spacious harbor, and its Danish neutrality, came to be regarded for a time as the region's most notorious port for ships flying the Jolly Roger. Samuel Bellamey, George Bond, William Teach, William Burke, and Tempest Rogers were all notorious freebooters who called at St. Thomas often, where they were always able to dispose of their prizes at a handsome profit. But the island had to pay a price for its exotic visitors in the form of an unsavory reputation over several decades.

In 1682, the French pirate Jean Hamlin captured several dozen vessels around Jamaica. May of the following year found Hamlin aboard his ship *La Trompeuse* at anchor in St. Thomas harbor, where he was granted refuge by Adolph Esmit, the island's notoriously corrupt governor. But the English wanted Hamlin badly. In early 1684, a certain Captain Carlisle of the British Navy aboard *HMS Francis*, cornered Hamlin in the harbor and burned *La Trompeuse*, sending a strong message to other freebooters.

Although St. Croix had less of a reputation for piracy and privateering, the island did attract a few robber luminaries, such as Jean Martel and Michel de Grammont (1645–86). It was while using St. Croix as his sometime base that the latter raided the coasts of Spanish South America in the late 1670s. More than a century later, the Robin Hood figure Roberto Cofresí (1802-25) roved the waters of eastern Puerto Rico and the Vieques Sound, preying in part on Danish shipping, before being captured in 1825 by U.S. Naval Capt. John Sloat, tried, and executed in El Moro in Puerto Rico in that same year. However, his name still resounds on many Hispanic lips on St. Croix to this day.

Is there anything good that might be said about this desperate lot? Aboard their own ships and going about their own business, they were actually rather democratic and fair-minded. Before heading out on a voyage, they drew up a set of articles for their governance at sea. A captain was selected on the basis of his record in hauling in loot, and he received a share in accordance with his performance. The crew agreed upon shares for everyone on board the vessel, and if the trip met with success, they divided things up equitably. Squabbles were handled judiciously. They developed a rudimentary form of insurance to protect themselves in the event of injury going about their trade. Among themselves they were generally as positive and rational as they were brutal toward their adversaries.

The broader perspective, however, presents a darker picture. There has never been a time in history when there were no pirates and the mayhem associated with them. The phenomenon occurs naturally wherever there are desperate men who seek their fortunes outside the limits of organized society and wherever there are trade goods and wealth exposed over lines of transit beyond the reach of authority. So it's a good bet that there will be pirates in this world for as long as there are vessels that ply the seas.

*Said to be Michel de Grammont,
St. Croix-based privateer.*

Ralph D. DeChabert, 1890–1955, journalist, labor union leader, and public servant on St. Croix.

CHAPTER 18

RALPH D. DECHABERT: JOURNALIST, NATIVE LEADER, GENTLEMAN

GEORGE TYSON, well-known Crucian historian and scholar, published a book last year that Virgin Islanders need to know about. Entitled *Searching for Truth and Justice: The Writings of Ralph D. DeChabert, 1915–1922*, this 118-page volume deals in great detail with the life and labor union activities of Ralph D. DeChabert, a native son of St. Croix who has for too long been relegated to the margins of Virgin Islands History.

Tyson's labors permit us to take a trip back through time and have a close look at a very important period in local history. DeChabert was an active participant in the creation and work of the St. Croix Labor Union, along with D. Hamilton Jackson, Ralph Bough, Casper Holstein, and Reginald Barrow. Like Jackson, DeChabert was a journalist who also founded his own newspaper, *The St. Croix Tribune*, in the struggle for workers' rights. Tyson has searched meticulously through that newspaper and selected all the important editorials and articles with relevance to the Labor Union movement on St. Croix and offered them, along with a careful analysis, to the reader. The result is a close-up look at the crucial events of the period 1916 to 1922.

Ralph D. DeChabert (1891–1955) was born on St. Croix on March 8, 1891, to Louis DeChabert and Laura Elodia Jackson. Louis was a clerk who lived with his family in a modest dwelling on Hill Street in Christiansted. When he died in 1894, Laura was forced to sell the house and take up work as a seamstress. Yet she remained an imposing figure in the lives of Ralph and his sister Florence, insisting that they attend school and take their education seriously.

Though his childhood was one of modest means, young Ralph made the most of his opportunities. In his early years, he became enchanted with reading, and as a young man he developed into an excellent writer. In his teens he took a job at the *St. Croix Avis* as a printer, which inspired his interest in journalism and current affairs. In his spare time, he studied Law by correspondence at the Extension Service of LaSalle University in Chicago. He also joined the Christiansted Mutual Improvement Society, founded by Dr. D.C. Canegata to promote study and discussion of ideas and events among the island's young men. From the beginning he was motivated by issues, ideas, and the life of the mind. Above all, his attention focused on the plight of the workers.

And there was a good deal to be concerned about at that time in the Danish West Indies. Those were the years of the decline of the Danish colonial presence in the islands, the subsequent sale of those islands to the United States, the formation and struggles of the labor movement, and the onset of U.S. rule under Naval administration. Not surprisingly, Ralph DeChabert became deeply involved while still a young man in both world affairs and local politics.

The Labor Union movement was the most recent in the long line of central events in local history that had begun with Abolition and extended through Emancipation (1848) to Fireburn (1878). In the early 1900s, the final event in that series occurred when The St. Croix Labor Union took the lead in the perennial struggle of the workers against the planter class. In January 24, 1916, the Union staged a strike for higher wages and better working conditions. The Planters resisted and work stopped on the estates. On February 26, the parties arrived at an agreement that settled the strike, giving the Union a victory. For the workers it was the first time they had ever prevailed against the planters and dealt with them face-to-face as equals.

Ralph DeChabert's intelligence, writing skills, and journalistic experience earned him, at the young age of twenty-five, the position of vice-president of the Union from 1916 to 1918, alongside the president, D. Hamilton Jackson (1884–1946), who had already made a successful trip to Denmark where he gained a hearing before the Danish national parliament. As a result of that success, he established a newspaper and eventually defied the local Danish administration. On the force of these achievements, Jackson quickly attained heroic status among the people of St. Croix.

But the positive relationship between the two men did not last long. After the settlement of the strike in 1916 that procured modest gains for the workers, Jackson's attention wandered. In early 1917, he journeyed to the States, with full support of the Union, to pursue legal studies. During his absence, DeChabert minded the shop, until 1919, when the leadership of the Union fell to him, a post he held until 1921. It wasn't long after that time that Jackson's attention turned entirely away from Union matters.

In the meantime, a second strike occurred in 1921 that was not nearly as successful as the first. The settlement led to rancor in the Union ranks. Jackson and his closest followers—Barrow, Holstein, and others—attempted to shift blame to DeChabert. Accusations flew back and forth. What actually happened has never been exactly established though Jackson clearly attempted to side-step blame for the outcome of the strike, a move that DeChabert bitterly protested. In fact, it was to combat Jackson and his followers that DeChabert founded *The St. Croix Tribune* in 1922 and maintained it with great passion until 1935.

Leaving the Union in 1921, DeChabert found much to occupy his many talents. From 1917 until 1931, The Territory of the Virgin Islands was under the newly imposed U.S. Naval rule. DeChabert vigorously protested Navy abuses and shortcomings in its treatment of the native population. His was a major voice for civilian government.

It was during this period that he met and married Ansetta Muckle, the indomitable "Miss Annie," a woman who knew the wages of selfless dedication and hard work. Together they created a home and raised a family of five children. They imbued their youngsters with a sense of discipline and a deep respect for education, producing a physician, a lawyer, a doctorate in language study, a school administrator, and a teacher. This was at a time when few Virgin Islanders ventured to the Mainland for education.

When civilian rule came to the Virgin Islands in 1931, DeChabert continued his life in public affairs. He held a position on the Colonial Council, where he served with distinction. Above all, he was instrumental in the drafting and passage of two landmark pieces of legislation—The Homestead Act (1932) and The Organic Act of 1936. After the latter law established a constitution-based government in the Virgin Islands, many opportunities opened to native Virgin Islanders, allowing them to hold an expanded number of government positions; DeChabert himself served in the positions of Tax Assessor and Recorder of Deeds.

The 1940s saw another change in his life-course; he became a farmer. In the post-Union days, several south-side estates had been acquired by former Harlem numbers racket king Casper Holstein. After Holstein's death, Syrian-immigrant businessman Joseph Alexander purchased the tracts in the early 1940s at auction and in turn sold them to Ralph DeChabert in 1945 for the sum of $23,000.00 on a down-payment of a thousand dollars and trust. The erstwhile journalist filled a long-time dream by developing the estates as a dairy and cattle farm, producing fresh milk for Christiansted and cattle for Puerto Rico. In this manner, Ralph DeChabert lived out the last ten years of his life as a hard-working farmer. He passed away at his residence on Queen Cross Street in Christiansted in 1955, leaving a balance of some $9,000.00 that he owed on the land at Jerusalem.

Ralph DeChabert left behind him an admirable record of achievement and a distinct imprint on his times. He showed himself to be a stalwart of his people and a refined gentleman in his dealings with everyone. But his influence was not yet spent. His widow "Miss Annie" struggled faithfully after his death to make the payments on the "land at Jerusalem," which by then supported only a modest herd of cattle. At times it seemed like a hopeless struggle. In 1962, however, oil baron Leon

Hess appeared out of nowhere and purchased the land for the building of The Hess Oil Refinery for a then considerable sum. Not only did that purchase and the refinery that it produced rocket the island into a period of unprecedented economic development, creating thousands of jobs and millions of tax dollars but the DeChabert family, under the prudent guidance of Ralph's oldest son, Dr. Ralph A. DeChabert, reinvested the purchase sum in the creation and development of Sunny Isle Shopping Center. That project became the focus for all the subsequent growth that has taken place in the central part of St. Croix, from that time to the present. The outcome of that venture sparked nothing less than an economic revolution.

So it has turned out that Ralph D. DeChabert's youthful dreams in 1916 of helping his people advance beyond the poverty of the cane fields and the long hours in the sugar factory at pitiful wages has been fulfilled in ways that would both astound and greatly please him.

The hand press used by DeChabert in his newspaper, The St. Croix Tribune.

A West Indian Maroon.

CHAPTER 19

MARRONAGE: THE FLIGHT TO FREEDOM

IN A PREVIOUS ARTICLE, we looked at the manner in which the lower, poorer elements of European society in the West Indies escaped from the many constraints of organized society in early colonial times by running off and joining the buccaneers. Few slaves could ever take advantage of that opportunity. However, another means was available to them to take leave from the harsh master of their servitude—marronage.

From 1672 until 1803, the Danish West Indian islands received around 100,000 captives from West Africa, destined to serve as laborers on the islands' plantations. Many lived and died in that condition. Some managed to buy their freedom. And others risked their lives and escaped from the system of bondage in one way or another by running away. Those escapees came to be called "Maroons." This is a bit of their story.

Historians have identified three varieties of marronage for the Virgin Islands during the colonial period, as well as for the broader Caribbean: petit marronage, grand marronage, and maritime marronage.

The life of an average slave on a Crucian plantation in the eighteenth century was by turns exhausting, boring, and oppressive. Though most found the means to adapt to it, some did not or could not. Such a slave might look for a propitious moment and then run away from the plantation, in some cases permanently, in others just to have a temporary break from the routine. The latter instance was called petit marronage.

In so doing, the runaway left behind a roof over his head, a regular supply of food, his comrades in the fields, and perhaps even his family, however oppressive those overall conditions of his life might have been. Moreover, he left in full knowledge that he would most likely be hunted down and subjected to a harsh punishment upon his capture, followed by a humiliating return to the estate. But the lure of freedom—even on a temporary basis—beckoned powerfully. So he picked his moment and slipped off into the bush and the unknown.

In petit marronage, the runaway did not necessarily venture far from his estate. He tried to find a location in the woods, perhaps near a neighboring plantation where trees and fruit would be available. He would also raid the peripheral gardens and with luck make off with a chicken or other small animals. He might even make contact with other slaves and get support from them on other plantations. But by the end of the day, he had to fend for himself. In a week or so, he might tire of sleeping in the open air, scrabbling for food, and hiding day and night in constant fear. Under such conditions, he might voluntarily return to his estate. It was sometimes the case that he could appeal to the master of a nearby estate to intercede for him with his own master.

The runaway's punishment depended on the length of his absence and the number of times that he might have already run away in the past. He could be whipped, put on restricted rations, stood in the stocks, or in extreme cases, mutilated. Multiple runaways were threatened with the loss of a leg. And then a second. The records contain the story of a certain Mingo, who lost both legs from frequent running away. But that penalty was not often imposed, largely because it would have diminished the slave's value as a piece of property. Sometimes owners preferred to sell such a recalcitrant slave to another plantation or dispose of him off-island in the inter-island slave trade rather than mutilate him, for by that means something could be saved of his monetary value. In time, petit marronage came to be regarded by the system as an annoyance that was simply a part of being in the sugar-producing business.

Grand marronage was another matter. In this variety of resistance, slaves attempted to run completely away from their plantations and form communities in remote, isolated parts of the island. In St. Thomas

MARRONAGE: THE FLIGHT TO FREEDOM

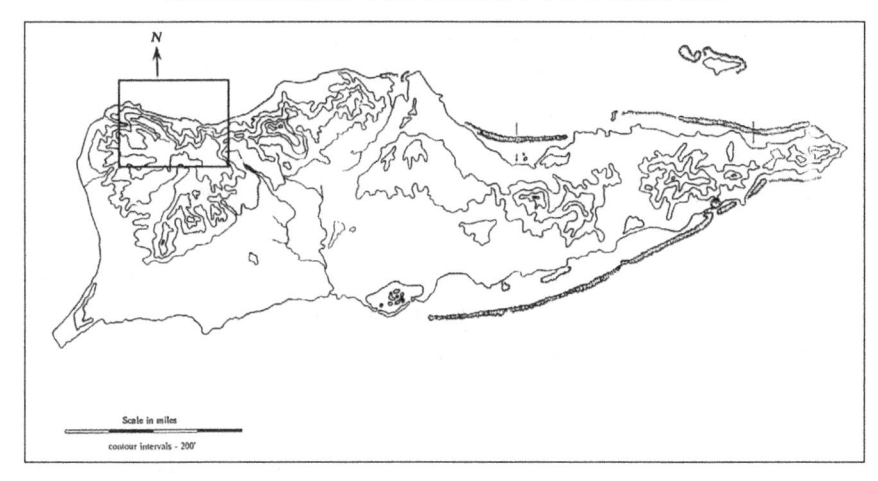

Map of St. Croix showing the Maroon Hills.

that was a difficult proposition due to the island's restricted size. In the larger, mountainous islands of the Caribbean—Jamaica, Haiti, Cuba, Española—however, grand marronage was altogether possible and common. Those islands came to hold large numbers of runaways whose presence was permanent in certain of the islands' areas and dangerous to the islands' rulers.

Because of its larger size, combined with rugged terrain, St. Croix afforded the opportunity to runaway slaves to form their own communities. In fact, a section of the northwestern quadrant of St. Croix still carries the name "Maroon Ridge" from that practice during colonial times. That area is mountainous and unsuited for plantations and the growing of sugarcane. Moreover, the northern slope extends precipitously and cliff-like down to the sea, rendering effective pursuit all but impossible. To those rugged extremes desperate slaves escaped and survived. It proved quite difficult to capture them once they had made it that far.

But planters were not without the means of combating the maroons. When maroon numbers grew too large, they would organize a "maroon hunt" (called a Battue), and then comb the island to drive them out into the open, at least in areas other than the Maroon Hills. The observant Moravian missionary C.G.A. Oldendorp notes in this regard that "Since the Free Negroes, who understand this business best of all, have trained dogs for such purposes, they are able to round them up like wild game."

The third type of escape was called "maritime marronage." This involved acquiring a vessel and actually leaving the island and slavery behind. The usual goal was to make it to Puerto Rico. Oldendorp tells us that: "In October of 1758 more than a hundred Blacks attempted to seize a vessel on St. Thomas and escape to Puerto Rico. Though they were thwarted in that plan, the failure did not hinder others from making the same attempt."

Numbers of slaves in St. Croix, however, had better opportunities for escape by sea, as recounted by the Danish planter Reimert Haagensen. "This island (Porto Rico) has brought many people to tears, for they and their entire families were ruined, when, in a single night, [25 to 30] of their slaves ... deserted to that place. It was in that way that the heirs of [Mr.] Bondwyn lost everything when all of their slaves ran away to that island in the course of a single night. The plantation had to be sold because of that."

From early in colonial history, Puerto Rico offered a great attraction to the enslaved of these islands. Events of August 1664 provide an excellent case in point. On that day three women and one man from the French colony on St. Croix stole a small canoe and made their way to the eastern shore of Puerto Rico. The locals wanted to sell them immediately for a quick profit, but the Governor of the island—Juan Pérez de Guzmán—intervened and extended to them the protection of the King of Spain. "It does not seem proper," he said, "that the king should reduce to slavery those people who take flight to seek his protection."

From that time it became the practice that if a slave arrived in Puerto Rico from these islands, he became a free man, provided he was willing to swear allegiance to the King of Spain and embrace the Catholic faith through baptism. Moreover, Puerto Rico was a large island with a good deal of undeveloped land and laborers were lacking.

MARRONAGE: THE FLIGHT TO FREEDOM

That simple formula opened the gates over the next century for a steady stream of freedom-seekers from St. Croix to the west. So many, in fact, dared to take that route that by the 1760s the Danish government complained loudly to Spain about the loss of manpower, with the result that in The Treaty of 1767, those nations agreed to seal off that escape route. Before the door was slammed shut, however, hundreds, perhaps even thousands of enslaved Africans in our islands drank by that means the sweet waters of freedom.

It is a well-known fact that African people in these islands forced their freedom from Denmark in 1848 by open revolt. What is lesser known is that large numbers of unknown individuals dared to take matters into their own hands in the two centuries before Emancipation and seize freedom on their own behalf and on their own terms by means of marronage. If you are looking for a good reason to celebrate Black History Month, here it is.

Virgin Islands Mocko Jumbies.

CHAPTER 20

CULTURE & CHANGE IN THE VIRGIN ISLANDS

EVERYONE TALKS ABOUT culture, but many would be hard-pressed to say exactly what it is. Some say you are born with it. Others think it is inherently related to race and color. Some others connect it with religion. What is culture and how does it relate to people and to the societies in which they live? In truth, there are probably as many definitions of culture as there are anthropologists and street corner philosophers.

To understand what culture is and how it functions, it must first be recognized that humans are social creatures. At the beginning of our history, we realized that we could survive better in groups than as isolated individuals. In so doing, humans came together in small groups to take on the world. In order to survive, it was quickly recognized that every such grouping had to satisfy distinct individual needs—for food, shelter, protection, order, procreation, and a satisfactory understanding of how the world works. The manner in which a given society responds to and meets these "societal" needs generates behaviors that establish the parameters of a given culture and imbues it with a distinctive character.

But how is it that there are many human cultures in the world instead of just one? This interesting question boils down to a very simple proposition. No two groups of people are configured the same in terms of size, geographic location, climate, relationships with other groups, sources of food, and the caprices of nature. This is just another way of saying that no two cultures can occupy exactly the same place on the planet and therefore be subject to exactly the same external environmental conditions. Compare, for example, the arctic that produced a particular fishing/hunting Eskimo culture with the deserts of North Africa that produced the Bedouin way of life, the Great Plains of North America that produced Amerindian horse cultures, the fertile river valleys of the Near East that produced Semitic agricultural societies, and jungles of Amazonia that produced Amerindian horticultural ones.

It might be said then that culture results from the creation of human behaviors that respond to the possibilities presented by environments and external conditions. Culture creation begins when such behaviors produce what anthropologists call "artifacts," of which there are two kinds—first, material artifacts, that is, physical things that people produce, such as arrow heads, transistors, and pieces of chalk, in fact, just about everything one might imagine that has been "made" by humans. And secondly, there is non-material culture, that is, behaviors that produce ideas, actions, and performances, items such as theories, songs, stories, dance steps, poems, traditions, and the like. The combined effects of these two types of artifacts give humans and the societies they inhabit a slight advantage in their response to nature's challenges and therefore a greater chance of success, survival, reproduction, and the projection of the individual and the group into the future.

The integration of cultural artifacts and human behaviors is central to the functioning of a given culture. It is one thing to identify all known artifacts and behaviors of a given culture but quite another thing to know how all the pieces fit together and interact. An understanding of this functionality is the province of the anthropologist and the sociologist.

We might posit, for example, that in Crucian culture there is quadrille dancing, scratch band music, madras head-ties, callalou and fungi, and the Crucian language, to name only a few. It remains, however, a far more complicated matter to understand how these elements, along with others, all fit together and interact to produce true Crucian cultural behavior. This process a born native learns easily and without self-consciousness by means of participation, imitation, and interaction from early in life with one's elders and peers. For a child enculturation comes naturally and easily. On the other hand, to perfect and master a culture completely later in life is an all but impossible undertaking. Imagine, for example, the difficulties one would face if confronted with the task of becoming "Chinese" at, say, the age of thirty. Or of a Chinese person trying to become a Crucian from that same point in life.

All culture begins with language. Think, for example, of trying to be a Crucian and speaking, say, French or German. It has been correctly said that language is the vehicle of culture, and to that end I have observed of late that young Crucians living stateside often reconnect with one another on Facebook in their nostalgic longing for home by using their versions of written Crucian. An American friend of mine commented that it looked like Greek to him. Precisely. A Crucian says it to other Crucians in Crucian a way that standard English simply cannot duplicate.

The production, preparation, and consumption of food is another key element in any given culture. Polynesians love poi, Germans long for sausage, North Africans delight in couscous, and Indians will take their curry any day. Most North Americans will not find a bowl of callalou and fungi very exciting. But place it in front of a hungry Crucian, and you have a portrait of a man in heaven. Add to that a plate of conch in butter sauce, with boiled ground provisions, fried plantains, a Johnny cake, a benye or two, a glass of sorrel, followed by a bowl of red grout covered with rich cream and, well, there you have Crucian culture nicely set on a table. In addition to its well-proven effects on the belly, it goes a long way in re-affirming identity.

A number of other elements of Crucian culture could be easily added to this short list without straining the imagination. In terms of physical dwellings, the distinctively modest, single-story, concrete block homes, surrounded by crotons, hibiscus, and bougainvillea come immediately to mind. The norm inside such a dwelling is the matricentric model, in which, if not in the ruling position, the mother is at the least the focal point of the household. She presides over an extended family in which everyone seems to be a cousin or an auntie. The family group is generally highly religious, with a dash of jumbies and strong belief in the other world thrown in for good measure. Quelbé music and dance—at one time the Quadrille—are strong elements in the social cement that gives delight and binds people together. Mocko Jumbies can be counted on to appear at most festive occasions. And of course, the picture would not be complete without the Crucian story-teller, or tradition-bearer, recounting the misadventures of Bru Nansi and his cohorts.

And then there are the numerous idiosyncrasies of the culture that are almost too common to notice. The careful observer notes that these are folks who love a day at the beach but often don't venture into the water above their knees. These same folk are quick to invite you to their table and offer you a heaping plate of food, in a display of culinary generosity that often stuns outsiders. And yet paradoxically they display at the same time an uncanny wariness of authority and of the powers that be. And don't make the mistake to get caught in the crossfire when someone is "throwin' words." It takes all of these elements and thousands of others of similar miniscule nature to just begin to understand the complexity of this culture.

Cultures generally give the impression of being stable and unchanging. An element of truth resides in this observation, at least at the core of things cultural. At the same time, however, cultures are constantly changing, some slowly, some at incredible speeds. Anyone who doubts this has only to compare St. Croix in 1960 or so, with the St. Croix of today. It is readily apparent that "a plate of real food" of years past, for example, is slowly giving way to the mighty hamburger. The youth who once danced to scratch band music and Milo and the Kings now roll exclusively to hip-hop. Traveling locals today end up in Houston or Atlanta instead of St. John or St. Thomas. Moonlit gatherings under the taman tree have been replaced by isolated individuals each on his own cell phone, texting, sexting, and otherwise. Innocent school-yard squabbles that were at one time resolved by pushing and a few bad words, are now increasingly resolved, most unfortunately, by guns and knives.

While it is normal to decry the loss of culture and a shared past, it is at the same time inevitable that such loss does and will continue to occur. Even the most conservative culture undergoes change. Travel, innovation, invention, immigration, rejection of older norms and the acceptance of new ones, and contacts between different peoples and groups provide the impetus for that change. The resulting rapid transformation and the inability to adjust to it effectively often leads to transitional dissonance, a dilemma in which individuals attempt to hold onto culture in transformation while at the same time embracing new forms as a matter of necessity. As an example, we have enshrined Quadrille dancing here on St. Croix, rolling it out now almost exclusively on special occasions, whereas the youth have abandoned it completely for other forms of music and dance. Living with such contradictory modes focuses our consciousness on the past and renders it difficult to clearly understand what is occurring in the present.

In the final analysis, the fullness and diversity of human activity as we know it—literature, poetry, science, technology, romantic love, family life, the taste of wine, the sound of music, and just about everything imaginable—are all generated by different cultures in different manners. It is for this reason that we all participate in the human drama of human life. A close look at the rich cultural creations of the people of this small island in the Caribbean Sea sets in relief one sparkling tile in the grand mosaic of the human cultural life of our planet.

Local dancers doing the Quadrille, a Crucian cultural dance.

The British steamer La Plata *riding out the tsunami in the St. Thomas harbor.*

CHAPTER 21

TSUNAMIS: THE SCOURGE OF THE SEAS

THE GREAT WALLS of water that struck the lands of the Indian Ocean in 2004 and this past year in Japan are witnesses to the immense force of nature. In both those events, a seismic movement in the earth's crust at the bottom of the sea triggered a dislocation of water at the surface and thereby unleashed enormous waves that leveled everything in their paths. The 2004 event released a force equivalent to 23,000 atomic bombs and killed more than 150,000 people in 11 countries, making it the worst tsunami-type disaster in human history. It has been all but forgotten that just such a tsunami struck both St. Thomas and St. Croix in 1867, causing enormous damage. Moreover, the threat of just such another great wave remains with us.

A tsunami is created by an earthquake on the sea floor. That seismic activity pushes the earth's crust up vertically and out horizontally, in the process displacing a great quantity of water in the form of a gigantic wave that can achieve the surface speeds of a jet aircraft. Powered by such mass and velocity, the tsunami becomes an irresistible force, moving rapidly away from its epicenter in all directions. Such a wave of some 30 feet in height will destroy everything in its path.

Underwater tremors and earthquakes are quite common in the waters around Puerto Rico and the Virgin islands. The seismic activity for a typical month may register over a hundred of these. But most of them are minor tremors. Frequently, at least in geologic time, a full-fledged earthquake rocks the area, such as the 5.14 magnitude event that struck in the seabed north of Anegada and Virgin Gorda on April 13, 2011.

Though it caused some anxiety among locals, fortunately it did no damage and failed to generate a tsunami.

The Virgin Islands have not always been so lucky. During the afternoon of November 18, 1867, an earthquake of 7.5 magnitude occurred just north of the island of Anegada. Ten minutes after the first shock, a second shock struck. Both of these events sent out large waves of over 30 feet in height, moving at great speed. Some 10 minutes after the first shock, a large wave struck St. Thomas, entering the harbor at Charlotte Amalie, followed about 10 minutes later by a second wave.

Observers in the town witnessed a frightening scene. The first warning occurred when the water in the harbor receded dramatically, exposing the sea bottom and marine life for several hundred feet. Shortly afterwards, a large wave of some 35 feet entered the harbor and raced toward the shore. It left in its path a tangle of destroyed large vessels and smaller boats. Damaged but not sunk was the *U.S.S. De Soto* that was paying a port call at the island. A sister ship, the *U.S.S. Susquehanna* was not damaged.

Another large vessel, the *La Plata* of the Royal Mail Steamship Packet, was nearly capsized on its anchorage near the entrance to the harbor at Water Island. Sailors and some one hundred local workers who were provisioning the ship all scrambled wildly over the decks.

The wave then struck the waterfront with ferocity, destroying nearly all the buildings along the wharf and flooding others located further inland. Among the victims was the town's Iron Wharf. Schooners, steamships, sailing boats, and buoys were left stranded high and dry on the waterfront. The town was flooded to a level of 8 feet, extending inland a distance of some 250 feet. All in all, some four major waves hit the town, the most damaging being the second; the third and fourth waves were largely inconsequential. It was a major disaster by any measure.

Those same waves travelled rapidly across the open sea to the south and slammed into St. Croix. Minutes after that same strong earthquake shook the town of Frederiksted, two large walls of water crashed ashore, doing great damage to stores and warehouses on Strand Street. In just several minutes, much of the heart of the town was destroyed.

Those same waves carried the warship *U.S.S. Monongahela* of the United States West Indies Squadron into the town, and then the reflux carried her back onto the beach. Commander Bissell of the *Monongahela* had this to say about the event: "At 3 o'clock a terrible rumbling and vibration of the vessel was felt as if blowing off steam violently from the boilers: it was a very severe shock of an earthquake and lasted about a minute. Then a quiet occurred until two minutes past three when the water receded from the shore between Butler's Bay and Sandy Point with astonishing rapidity, and the island seemed approaching us. In a few seconds a reflux tide set in from seaward towards the land with such velocity as to carry this vessel and two others towards the beach."

Though the 227-foot-long *Monongahela* suffered only light damages, it was not until May 11, 1868, some five months later, that U.S. Naval engineers succeeded in refloating the vessel. She was then towed to Portsmouth, New Hampshire, where she underwent repairs. Two other American ships—a brigantine and a sloop—were also thrown onto land.

Given its severity, the tsunami claimed surprisingly few lives in Frederiksted. Feeling the strong quake and seeing the sea recede, many residents immediately fled inland to higher ground. A few, however, were not so lucky. Four sailors from the *Monongahela* lost their lives to the sea; one of them, Albert Vooseman, a 28-year-old mariner from Hamburg, Germany, was buried in the Anglican cemetery at St. Paul's Church where his grave can be seen today. An unknown Frederiksted woman was drowned as she collected wood near the salt pond. Recent research has shown that three women—Delphina Joseph, Agnes Miller, and a certain Petma [??]—are all listed in the St. Paul's Anglican burial register as having died of drowning on November 18, most likely from the tsunami.

Although protected by a long fringing reef, Christiansted was not spared the onslaught. After the earthquake, the townspeople witnessed

The U.S.S. Monongahela beached at Frederiksted.

a great wall of water rushing toward them from the north and promptly fled to higher ground. The wave pursued them nearly 200 feet inland, raising a frightening roar as it proceeded, audible miles away. Low-lying Gallows Bay was hardest hit, losing some twenty dwellings and all of the boats anchored in the bay.

All things considered, 1867 was a very a bad year for the Danish

TSUNAMIS: THE SCOURGE OF THE SEAS

West Indies. The most devastating hurricane in the islands' history to that point struck the islands on October 29, causing enormous damage. Twenty days later, the monster earthquake and tidal wave hit. In addition to these natural disasters, the islands were literally plagued by deadly endemic fevers. As a testimony to that pestilence, Admiral Palmer, commanding officer of the *De Soto*, died of Yellow Fever in December on St. Thomas, as had many others in that same year.

But it was the tsunami that had the greatest impact, occasioning the postponement of the local referendum set by the Danish government for the locals to voice their opinion on the recent U.S. offer to purchase St. Thomas. By the time that the vote was rescheduled and held in January of 1868, a new government was in place in the U.S., whose members promptly changed their minds about the acquisition, due in large part to the recent catastrophes. In this manner, the U.S. acquisition of the Danish West Indies was delayed some fifty years.

As bad as this misadventure may have been, things could get far worse. Scientists have for some time warned of the danger posed by a volcanic eruption on the island of La Palma in the Canary Islands that might well cause a mega-tsunami. Some such future seismic event would dislodge the summit's creviced western flank, called Cumbre Viaja, and cast it into the Atlantic Ocean. Twice the size of the Isle of Man, this mass of land would create a monster wave, which, by the time it hit our islands, would measure some 300 feet in height and travel at speeds in excess of 400 miles per hour. Such a catastrophic force would not only destroy all man-made structures in these islands, but it would reshape the islands geologically as well.

This gloomy but very possible scenario makes the tsunamis of 1867 look like a picnic and serves as yet another reminder that while man proposes, it is ultimately Nature that disposes.

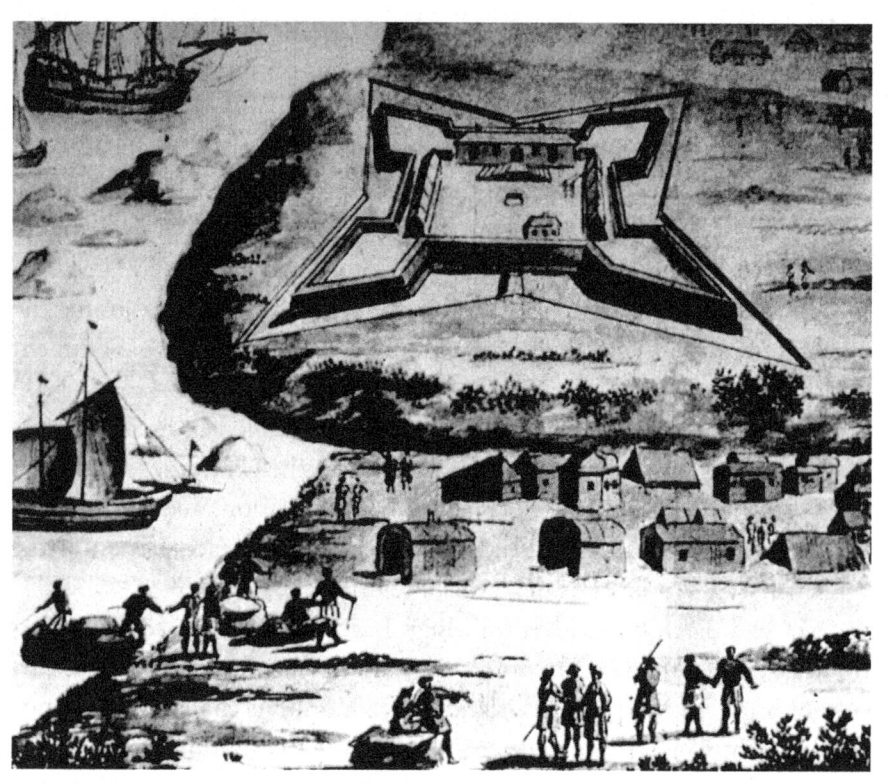

Gross Friedrichsburg, the Brandenburg slave trading fort on the Gold Coast, West Africa.

CHAPTER 22

A GERMAN WEST INDIES?: THE BRANDENBURGERS

EVERYONE IS FAMILIAR with the terms British West Indies and French West Indies. And in addition there have been the Dutch West Indies, the Spanish Indies and, of course, the Danish West Indies. But a German West Indies? It sounds preposterous, but it might well have happened.

Denmark took possession of St. Thomas in 1672 and established the Danish West India and Guinea Company to assume control of the island and administer it. The idea behind the move was to enter tropical agriculture, but in particular the production of tobacco, cotton, sugar, molasses, and rum. Contemporary mercantilist doctrine had it that every country needed to protect its stores of gold currency if it was to compete effectively in the war-torn world. In short, it needed hard currency to pay its armies. If, however, one nation had to buy, say, sugar from another country, then that transaction constituted a loss of bullion for the buyer and therefore resulted in military weakness that diminished the nation's ability to defend itself.

This hard logic led more than one European state to become involved in the struggle for colonies to provide a direct supply of tropical produce. For their part the Danes found that it was a difficult venture because they started late in the game. St. Thomas had an excellent harbor but little land that was useful for significant sugar production. From the start then, they attempted to trade Danish-produced goods for muscovado sugar, which they would then ship back to Copenhagen for sale on the Danish and north European markets.

SEA GRAPES AND KENNIPS

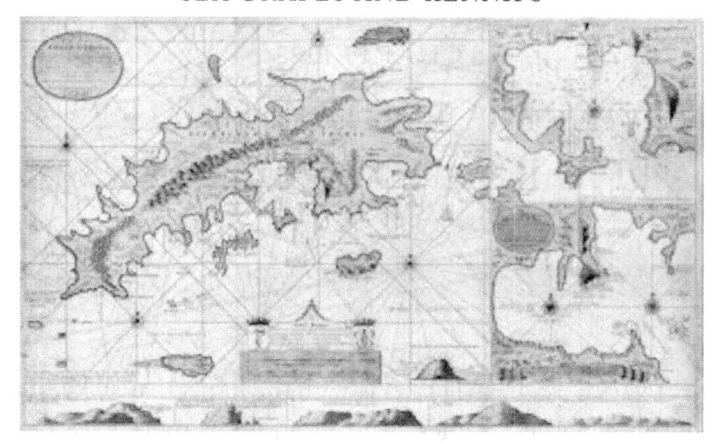

Map (1719) by Gerard van Keulen showing St. Thomas and its harbor at the end of the Brandenburg presence there.

This maneuver was easier said than done. St. Thomas was far from Denmark, and it took from six months to a year to complete the communication circuit between colony and home country. Governors of the island therefore were seduced into tempting illegal activities, such as dealing with pirates and collecting booty. Often they acted in an arbitrary, authoritarian manner in regard to their settlers, causing no little discord.

Adolph Esmit was one such governor from 1682 to 1684 and again in 1688. His commerce with privateers and his high-handed behavior led him to fall into disrepute with the Danish West India Company and the Danish King. Gabriel Milan (1684–1686), Esmit's replacement, proved to be even worse. He immediately overstepped his commission by dealing with pirates and engaging in illicit trade practices. St. Thomas soon became notorious as the most corrupt island in the Caribbean. Milan was eventually recalled to Denmark, tried for treasonous behavior, and then unceremoniously beheaded.

By the 1680s, Denmark had good cause to rethink its Caribbean enterprise and look about for a possible exit. One such opportunity was offered by the Great Elector Friedrich Wilhelm of Brandenburg, a principality located at the heart of what was to later to become the

A GERMAN WEST INDIES?: THE BRANDENBURGERS

modern state of Germany. In 1682, Brandenburg established the Brandenburg Africa Company to enter the seemingly lucrative slave trade on the Gold Coast of West Africa in what today is Ghana. From their forts, Gross Friedrichsburg, held from 1682 to 1717, and Arquin, they traded European goods for slaves and ivory. It soon became apparent that they needed an island in the Caribbean from which to sell slaves effectively, and so they began to cast about.

To their disappointment there were no more vacant islands available. So they arranged a deal with the Danish West India Company through the entrepreneur Benjamin Raule to lease sections of St. Thomas for a factory and a plantation in exchange for an annual fee and duties on imported Africans. In addition to the income, the Danes felt they would benefit from the increased commercial activity and, in particular, from the introduction of Africans into the island to augment the local labor force. In was under these conditions that the Brandenburgers entered into a thirty-year lease with the Company to extend from 1685 to 1715. Their section of the town came to be called the Brandenburgery.

It would have surprised no one at that time to suppose that in ten years time the Brandenburgers might well have taken over the entire island of St. Thomas because Denmark had soured on the idea of running a tropical colony. That Danish disposition resulted in the leasing of Company operations on the Gold Coast from 1689 to 1694 to Danish entrepreneur Nicholas Arff. And in 1690, the Company leased the entire island of St. Thomas to wealthy Norwegian merchant and financier Jørgen Thormohlen, an arrangement that lasted until 1694.

As it turned out, by the mid-1690s, the Danish Company re-assumed control over its possessions and struggled to make a go of them. The Brandenburgers retained their lease but quarreled with the Danish Company over several nagging issues. The Brandenburgers had refused to operate a plantation which would have provided the Danish Company with tax revenues. They continued to attract privateers which threatened the Company's good standing with Spain. The competition in the supply of European goods to the Danish settlers led to a fear of a

Brandenburg takeover. Finally, the Brandenburgers refusal to pay taxes and fees led the Company governor to break into their warehouse and seize goods. All these frictions made it extremely difficult to renew the lease in 1693. In that same year, the Company took back the Brandenburgery, and the determination of the Germans began to decline.

During those troubled times the Brandenburgers considered taking possession of several Caribbean islands, including Crab Island (Vieques), Peter Island in the BVI, Tortola, Tobago, and St. Croix just after the French abandoned it in 1696. But none of those efforts bore fruit. Nor were the Germans able to pry St. Thomas from Danish hands. When the lease expired in 1715, the Brandenburger warehouses were all but empty, and they were quite willing to give up the effort.

It is interesting all the same to speculate about what might have happened had they succeeded in making St. Thomas a German colony. Might a German-Caribbean Creole language have evolved in place of the Dutch and English Creoles? And how might German music— Mozart, Beethoven, and Wagner—have fared under the influence of African elements? And might there have occurred a migration to the Brandenburg cities of Emden and Berlin resulting in Caribbean communities there? And how might the United States have dealt with a German colony and naval base sitting astride the sea lanes on a major approach to the Panama Canal as World War One broke out?

German influence in the Danish West Indies did not come to an end with the departure of the Brandenburgers from St. Thomas in 1715. In the early 1730s, dozens of German missionaries arrived in the islands to found and operate the Moravian Mission churches in all three islands, an effort that extended well into the mid-nineteenth century, resulting in the conversion of thousands of Africans to the Moravian faith. German-speaking missionaries and officials—August Spangehberg, Count Ludwig von Zinzendorf, Friedrich Martin, Jakob Böhner, and many others—flowed into the islands and left their strong cultural imprints on individual believers and on the society. It is therefore not surprising that the most important book on the history and culture of the Danish

A GERMAN WEST INDIES?: THE BRANDENBURGERS

Moravian settlement at New Herrnhut on St. Thomas.

islands in the eighteenth century was written by a German, the Missionary Inspector Christian George Andreas Oldendorp.

The final episode of German influence in these islands was a curious but very significant one, changing the course of the Danish islands' history. After German unification around the core of Brandenburg-Prussia in 1848, that nation quickly became the dominant power in Europe. As the continent moved inexorably toward World War One, the United States grew apprehensive that Denmark would fall under German influence or perhaps even direct control and that as a result the Danish West Indies might become a foothold in the hemisphere for growing German naval power. This question became all the more crucial when the Panama Canal was opened in 1914. It was in this sense that the perceived German threat spurred the United States to give Denmark no choice but to sell the islands, which directly became the U.S. Virgin Islands.

The German presence and influence in the Virgin Islands have been eventful and lasting over the lengthy stretch of history from 1686 to 1916. However, for all their energy and ambitions neither individual Germans nor the German states were ever able to claim territory and establish a German West Indies.

Terra cotta Akan head.

CHAPTER 23

THE SPIRIT OF THE AKAN NATION IN ST. CROIX

VIRGIN ISLANDERS ARE generally aware of the Danish, Scottish, Irish, and English backgrounds of their history. There is of course also a strong African element about which a good deal is known in its general parameters. Specifics, however, are sometimes lacking, with some teachers and writers focusing on Egypt, Nubia, Ethiopia, and everywhere in between, none of which has any direct connection with our islands. Where then should one look to find the direct African antecedents to Virgin Islands history and culture? The Akan people of West Africa is an excellent place to start. Moreover, their introduction into the Danish West Indian islands beginning in the early eighteenth century has been well documented by historians.

Today some twenty million Akan people constitute the majority populations of Ghana and Ivory Coast in West Africa. They share a common culture and language, the latter called Akan, or Twi-Fante, a member of the Kwa family of African languages. The language has been written since colonial times in English script, but in 1978 an orthography was established in which all the dialects of Akan can now be written.

Elements of Twi found their way into a number of Caribbean languages, including Jamaican and Crucian. In the latter we have inherited a considerable stock of words, such as tan-tan, "a type of tree"; ba-ba, "a baby"; bomba, "a slave driver"; and a number of others. We also have interesting calques, or derivatives, such as "eye-water" for tears and so on.

The Akan people originated in the African Sahel and migrated south over the course of several centuries to the Atlantic coast. That process began with the establishment in the eleventh century AD of the

Palace of the Asantehene in Kumasi.

Kingdom of Bonoman, which was founded on trade relations between the Akan and neighboring peoples, including those at Timbuktu and Bornu. The discovery and successful mining of gold in their domains in the thirteenth century provided the impetus for the expansion of the Akan state and its differentiation into a number of daughter kingdoms. The best known among these were the kingdoms of Asantei and Akwamu, along with the Denkyira, Coromontin, Fante, and Ndyuka, to mention only a few among several dozen.

Akan kingdoms, such as the Asante, or Ashanti, were presided over by kings called the Asantehene. In former times, this king ruled over the powerful Asante Empire from its capital city of Kumasi, today with a population of about 1.4 million people. From there, he held sway over nearly all of the Gold Coast. Since independence in 1957 made Ghana into a republic, the role of the king has become mainly ceremonial though he remains a person of great prestige.

Although little of the Akan political system survived the Atlantic

THE SPIRIT OF THE AKAN NATION IN ST. CROIX

passage to our islands, distinct ethnic identities did and were clearly identified by colonial authorities, especially in the records of the Moravian Church and by such writers as C.G.A. Oldendorp. Another source is George Tyson's massive and invaluable *St. Croix African Roots Project.* As one example of this presence, the prominent role of the Akwamu people in the St. John revolt of 1733–34 has long been recognized by scholars.

Europeans were impressed by the gold-producing and gold-working abilities of the Akan people, and therefore they called the area the "Gold Coast." Over several hundred years, Danes and others exported a good deal of gold from that region, along with ivory and slaves. The abilities of the Akan people in the working of gold into fine pieces of art was widely acknowledged from early colonial times. That same appreciation of gold was carried across the Atlantic to these islands by the unfortunate captives in the trade and remains present today in our lingering fascination for the royal metal, especially in the form of wrist bracelets and earrings.

Akan society was organized on the basis of lineages, that is to say, lines of descent from a supposed common ancestor. Those lineages were said to be matrilineal in that descent passed from the mother to her children. The mother's brother, or the children's maternal uncle, played a central role in the lives of her offspring, largely displacing the biological father. Yes, the father recognized his children but he often had many of them, generated by the polygamous relations which he enjoyed.

Traces of these practices are to be seen today in modern Crucian society. First, households usually center on the mother and her role in raising the children in a society that is sometimes called matrifocal even though the overall society today is patrilineal as a result of European influences. Second, some Crucian men take pride in practicing a modified form of polygamy, in which they have "outside women" and "outside children" in addition to their primary family based on official marriage. These African survivals sometimes collide with European norms and morals, resulting a certain dissonance across the society.

Children born into Akan families receive their names in accordance with a unique naming system. Eight days after his birth, a male child is given a name for the day of the week on which he was born. Here are the names for the seven days of the week, listed Monday through Sunday: Kojo, Kwabena, Kwaku, Yaw, Kofi, Kwame, and Kwesi. A parallel system of names is likewise available for female children, namely: Adjoa, Abena, Akua, Yaa, Afua, Ama, and Akosua. At that same time, the child is given a second name, generally taken from an admired individual in the community or a prominent ancestor. Later, the youngster receives two more names, one usually from the Bible, among Christian families and the other from his father. The first two of these four names are those by which the child is known in the home and the latter two, in the outside world.

This Akan naming system has been all but lost in present-day St. Croix, a process that began in colonial times. Early Crucians sometimes used the practice of weekday names, usually on an informal basis. The names of admired ancestors and fathers, however, were generally lost because of the restrictive nature of the Danish colonial society. But the Moravians and other missionaries insisted on a biblical name—Nathanial, Ezekiel, Johannes, or the like—which, in the existing slave society, was generally the only name that the individual had. Though some weekday names do still appear occasionally even today, the Akan naming system was fairly well corrupted by its collision with slavery. One response to that loss, in my opinion, has been that some Caribbean parents bestow African or Arabic-sounding names such as Shakia, Keisha, Neisha, Tamika, Kareem, Malik, and so forth on their children in an apparent response to complete Europeanization.

In Akan areas, food production was based squarely on horticulture. A man owned a tract of land on which he had his dwelling, grew his crops, and tended his animals. Families lived relatively well on a diet of plantains, bananas, cassava, fruit, yams, and other tubers, along with meat and fish. This system transferred successfully if not completely to the plantations of the Danish West Indies. Every newly arriving African was allotted a small tract of land known as "provision ground," on which he was expected to produce a significant percentage of his own food. He used his African farming traditions to make the most of this limited land resource. This small-plot gardening continued throughout the colonial period, with traces lingering on even to the present time.

Slavery flourished in Akan areas even before the coming of the Europeans and Arabs. Generally, it has been referred to as household slavery as opposed to the plantation variety as practiced by Europeans in the Caribbean. It was a generally accepted practice and explains, in part, the apparent lack of conscience about selling other Africans to slave traders. Moreover, the system died only slowly and grudgingly. After their victory in the Third Ashanti War in 1874, the British forced the abolition of slavery on the Gold Coast kingdoms, some forty years after the British Emancipation Act of 1833.

Slavery, however, remained difficult to eradicate among the Akan even after abolition. Trokosi, or the enslavement of young girls for the use of temple priests, remains in practice to this day, in spite of efforts to expunge it. So does the sale of young boys to fishermen and farmers in the area of Lake Volta, where youths as young as six-years-old, are subjected to a brutal form of servitude.

Akan culture, long before its acceptance of Christianity and Islam, was home to a thriving spiritual life. A single, great God called Nyame, presided over his creation from the distant heavens. Under him, lesser gods resided in rivers, streams, forests, mountains, lakes, trees, and in all forms of life. In addition, numerous other spirits abounded not only in the other world but in this world as well. Last but not least, there were the spirits of the deceased ancestors who remained in close contact with the living and who acted as a kind of bridge between them and the enormous power latent in the world beyond. It was the shaman-priest who understood these matters and acted as the conduit between the living in this world and the gods, spirits, and ancestors in the world that lies beyond.

Remnants of this world view are to be seen in present-day St. Croix.

Though it is hidden from daily view, Obeah is said to be widely believed in and practiced still, replete with the machinations of the occasional Obeah man and Obeah woman. It is not uncommon here that spirits and ancestors are called upon to lend their considerable leverage to the projects of the living. Similarly, jumbies are felt to be everywhere, busy working their mischief on the naïve and the unsuspecting. A knowledge of their ways is required to diminish the effects of their caprices. In these affairs the hand of the African Motherland remains strong and alive.

A bold oral literature has long flourished on the Gold Coast. It centers on the half-man, half-spider deity known as Anansi, who, among other feats, introduced the practice of storytelling to humanity. As tradition has it, this crafty trickster talked Nyame, the Great Sky God, into allowing him access to all the stories that the god had securely locked away. From that day forward, the Akan people heard these magnificent tales and then retold them time after time, producing a variegated corpus of oral literature.

These tales traveled readily across the Atlantic in the minds and memories of those unfortunate enough to have become entangled in the slave trade. As a result the Anansi stories quickly spread all over the Caribbean, including of course St. Croix, where they remain an active, creative force to this day.

Music and dance have always been far more than a mere pasttime for the Akan. When one approaches an Akan king in his court, for example, it is with particular movements of the body, hands, and feet set to drum and music as specified in a prescribed ritual. The entire society is permeated with such ritual dances that are required by custom and performed as a regular part of daily life.

The essence of the Akan music traditions was carried across the Atlantic in the pulse of the djembe drum. Not many such drums were physically transported on ships to the islands during the trade, but it is certain that the concept of those drums was very much alive in the minds of the enslaved and that real drums were soon constructed from the design pattern in those ideas. In that transaction, the essence of West African music was reborn in St. Croix and other islands, and it soon established its own identity in the Quadrille, Lancers, field songs, seasonal celebrations, Kareso, and the like. It is in this realm of music, song, and dance that the influence of Mother Africa in St. Croix resonates most clearly and confidently.

The Akan realms of West Africa date back into the past nearly a thousand years. In their long history, they have survived invasions, war, colonialism, slavery, and the initial trials of independence. In that long process, they forged a unique culture that still can boast many creations of substance, beauty, and longevity. Not least, this culture contributed well over a million souls to the New World Diaspora, many thousands right here in St. Croix. For anyone wishing to know and understand the African element in Virgin Islands history and culture, here is the place to begin.

*Stanley Jacobs, founder, flutist, and leader of the
Ten Sleepless Knights.*

CHAPTER 24

MASTERS OF QUELBE: STANLEY & THE TEN SLEEPLESS KNIGHTS

THERE IS A BATTLE going on in the Virgin Islands today. It goes largely unnoticed but it is a battle all the same. Like many of the struggles these days, it involves culture. On the one side there is hip hop, rap, and other imported forms of musical expression, along with Reggae, Bachata and Salsa. Its champions are the young, the alienated, and the sometimes directionless. On the other side of the fray, we hear the sounds of Quelbe, Quadrille, and Scratch Band music. Its proponents number an older generation of Crucians, tradition bearers, men whose entire lives have been steeped in Crucian culture, men like Stanley Jacobs and the Ten Sleepless Knights, Jamsie Brewster and the Happy Seven, Sylvester "Blinky" McIntosh and the Roadmasters, Joe Parris and the Hotshots, Bully Petersen and the Kafooners, Doc Petersen, Dmitri Copeman, and others.

Traditional Crucian music traces its roots far back into the 18th century. At the very beginning there were only the field songs, imported directly from the African tradition and sung by the plantation workers as a means of communicating the burden of their lowly position and of lightening the load of their labor. After the workday ended and on holidays, those same workers fled into the nearby woods and with a range of drums and other percussion instruments, danced to the rhythms of repressed hopes and dreams of survival.

Things very rarely remain the same for long. So it was with early Crucian music. In time, the field workers came into direct contact with European masters and European plantation workers and missionaries, and they were thereby introduced to new influences. The Europeans needed musicians to play for the balls and special occasions, and from that, the Crucians adopted new instruments—the guitar, banjo, fife, flute, and such to add to their several drums, especially the Bamboula and the Goumbey. They also picked up new melodies from Quadrille and Lancers tunes and from European folk music. But to these new forms they added a distinctive African-Crucian element in the form of catchy drum rhythms and in the introduction of an entirely new language, its pronunciation and unique intonation. Crucian music was born from that union.

There are numerous curious examples of the manner in which the music of these two cultures coalesced, creating a new musical form. One plantation owner, for example, felt so deprived of music that he recruited a group of Crucians to assemble just outside his bedroom window every morning to play his favorite music as he arose to face the day. These were obviously European tunes but played in an African manner, resulting in an obvious new syncretic creation. Similar little bands also played on special occasions—festive celebrations, balls, birthdays, and the like. And a small band was usually assembled on the plantation to accompany the master on the road marches that took place during the Christmas season.

In time, these bands became a regular part of plantation life. They developed their own instrumentation, evolved a particular style of play, and often wrote their own songs. These latter centered on specific individuals, events, and incidents and quickly became an accepted part of local tradition and culture, both inside the plantation house and out.

By the twentieth century these bands had come to be known by several names—Quelbe bands, Scratch bands, or Quadrille bands. However slight there differences might have been, they all shared a common origin as well as the conviction that they were neither European nor African in essence but uniquely Crucian in form, content, and aesthetic expression. It was into this world that a young Stanley Jacobs stepped in the 1960s.

STANLEY & THE TEN SLEEPLESS KNIGHTS

Stanley and the Ten Sleepless Knights. STANDING: *Eldred Christian; Dr. Lauren Larsen; Tino Francis; Kendell Henry; and Harold Johnson.* KNEELING: *Stanley Jacobs; Gilbert Hendricks; & Christian Thompson.*

As a result of his own origins and background, Stanley brought yet another element to the genre—he was completely bilingual and bicultural in Crucian and Spanish. He was born at Isabel Segunda in Vieques on October 29, 1941, to Juana Saldaña Jacobs and was brought to St. Croix as an infant two months later. His father Raymond Jacobs had been a photographer who was hired by the U.S. Navy to take pictures of the naval installations in Vieques and Culebra. Arriving in St. Croix, the young Stanley became a Crucian quite quickly, living in Christiansted, in the Schjang Yard, and then in Gallows Bay. His completely bilingual and bicultural background rendered a bowl of callalou as tasty to him as a plate of lechón with seasoned rice, maduros, and tostones, in the same manner as a round of music from a scratch band was as seductive to him as Puerto Rican Salsa and Plena. He attended grade school in the old Steeple Building School, then later enrolled at the Christiansted Grammar School, and finally at the High School, graduating in 1959. Thereafter, he went directly to Lincoln University, from which he graduated in 1963 with a BA in Psychology.

With war in Vietnam looming, Stanley was drafted into the Army in 1963 right after graduation. He served in the division of Chemical, Biological, and Radiological Warfare at Edwards Arsenal in Washington, D.C., until his honorable discharge from military service in 1966, fortunately allowing him to avoid a tour in Vietnam. At that point he decided that his future lay, not in the jungles of the Far East, but at home in St. Croix so he returned there the same year as his discharge.

Once back home, Stanley fell into the local music scene that he had always admired as a child and young person. Playing the fife first and later the flute, he found a place in the Simmonds Brothers Band. At that time, the Quelbe bands were for the most part pre-electrical, featuring instrumentation whose roots extended far back into the past, namely the sardine pan guitar, the guitar, banjo, and fife, accompanied by the drum, squash, steel, wash-pan, pipe, or ass-pipe, and the mirambola, a kind of box with a bass output. Led by Stanford Simmonds, the band was not destined for a long life. Stanley was invited shortly thereafter to play a "pump flute," in the Joe Parris Band.

After those short stints, Stanley decided with some of his friends in the group to start their own band around 1970, which they originally called "The Vikings." In a short time, that name was transformed by one of the original band members, Pierpoint Petersen, who joked that he had ten sleepless nights because he had ten children. Fellow band member Eldred "Edgie" Christian proposed that the band's name be changed to "Stanley and the Ten Sleepless Knights" and the name stuck, enduring over the past forty-two years. During that time, some forty individuals have played in the band but only three remain from the original group—Petersen, Christian, and Stanley Jacobs himself.

Over those forty years, the band has dedicated itself to playing numerous Quelbe tunes from the past, thereby keeping a long cultural tradition alive and thriving. During that long span, individual members have written original songs and developed them musically, including tunes such as "The Butcher and the Politician" and "Vietnam" by Stanley along with a half dozen songs by Stanley and Edgy Christian. And other distinguished band members have likewise written numerous well-known tunes, including Tito Francis and others with songs such as "General Buddhoe," "Freedom," "Broncojig," "Bulljig," and others.

Stanley Jacobs has dedicated the last forty odd years of his life to playing and singing the music of St. Croix to some three generations of Crucians. What changes has he noted in the music over that long span? First, he has seen a pronounced change in the instrumentation and its method of play. At the beginning of his voyage, the instruments were relatively simple, fabricated, for the most part, by the musicians themselves by hand. The early guitars and banjos originated as "sardine cans" to which strings and necks were attached, just as the finger-holes of the fifes and flutes were drilled into bamboo, then called "wild cane" and into metal pipes. Drums were often made by pulling a goatskin over a barrel, as was the practice of the legendary Frank Charles. A simple piece of iron could be struck by another piece of iron to produce a rhythmic beat while a length of steel could be shaped into a triangle. A squash was simply hollowed out and left to dry, becoming a raspy wiro. And a washtub bass could be fashioned by affixing to it a broomstick, attached to a length of rope. Finally, an ass-pipe, or tailpipe, was removed from a derelict car and blown into by a strong set of lungs, producing a distinctive reverberating bass sound.

Big changes occurred in the 1970s and 1980s, when musicians could purchase commercially made instruments, such as electric guitars and pianos, saxophones, high quality banjos, drum sets, conga drums, and powerful amplifiers. At that point both the band and the music that it produced went through significant alterations, in which the early bands that produced a relatively small sound were transformed into units that could easily produce a very large one. The advent of modern instruments and their electrification established a critical juncture in the long history of Quelbe.

With those innovations came another significant change—the band and its music began to travel. Curiously, the music came to be greatly admired and adopted first in St. Thomas. Stanley reminisces that they often played more frequently at St. Thomian venues and events than at those in St. Croix.

Equally curious was the change that occurred in the general manner in which the enhanced Quelbe music and its musicians were received by the general public. Stanley notes that back in the 1950s and 1960s there existed a certain stigma attached to playing local music, and that it was only some twenty to thirty years later that the negative associations began to disappear. Slowly, Quelbe came to be known as "heritage music," and along with that recognition appeared a measure of admiration, respect, and celebration of cultural pride for both the genre and its musicians. To mark those honors, in 2005, the Legislature of the Virgin Islands passed a resolution naming Quelbe the official music of the Virgin Islands, singling out Stanley and the Ten Sleepless Knights and Blinky and the Roadmasters for special recognition. It was long in coming but well deserved.

Special attention arrived from another quarter as well. Not only did Denmark produce a St. Croix inspired musical group, The Polcalypso Band that pumped out remarkably good Quelbe music, but moreover, a number of invitations were extended from that country to Stanley, Jamsie, and Blinky to travel to Scandinavia to share their musical treasures with thousands of appreciative Danes. Stanley made treks there in 2005, 2008, and 2011, each time increasing his popularity and receiving greater critical praise. It should be noted here that for many years Stanley, Jamsie, and Blinky have shared the throne of Quelbe musical culture equitably together and in mutual appreciation of one another's talents and achievements.

Stanley has now been at it for some forty-odd years. When asked about a rumor that he will step down at the end of the present year, he simply shrugged it off. He is a man of no double-talk and very few excuses and complaints. His one dissatisfaction at this point in his life is that Quelbe music has not been fully embraced in the school curriculum with an eye for preparing the next generation to take over the helm and continue the tradition of the Crucian musical and cultural heritage into the future. In this he has a good point.

The justification for such a plan is to be found in the genius of the music itself. When they hear Stanley's band pumping out rhythms and melodies that float over the soft tropical air on an especially good night, or when they are awakened at four in the morning at Christmas time by the band making its way through the streets on a flatbed, singing about the delights of guavaberry and a piece of pork for Christmas, or when they catch the sounds of a wonderfully played, longtime favorite song, Crucians can only throw their heads back and render the highest possible compliment: "That music sweet me up, boy!" And indeed, the irresistible rhythms, the compelling, sweet, sweet melodies, and the Crucian words that knit the past and present so intimately together, all of that does inevitably sweet us up, moving the heaviest of feet to dance, lightening the saddest of hearts to renewal, and lifting the most elusive of souls to head-spinning heights. That is the real remuneration that has kept Stanley and the Ten Sleepless Knights on the bandstand for the past forty years. And if I had my way, they would be there for at least another forty and then some.

Christopher Columbus

CHAPTER 25

REVISITING THE COLUMBUS LANDING ON ST. CROIX, NOVEMBER 14, 1493

INTRODUCTION

SOME YEARS AGO, on November 12, 2000, at a lecture given at the University of the Virgin Islands, my longtime friend and valued colleague Attorney W. Geigel first advanced the idea that the Columbus landing on St. Croix of November 14, 1493, actually took place on either the southern or western shore of the island rather than at the more generally accepted site of Salt River. Several years later, in 2005, he developed that thesis further in a small book entitled, *Salt River in St. Croix: Columbus Landing Site?* And more recently, in November of 2011, he lectured on the same theme, curiously enough, during a celebration of that event, this time at Salt River. In the course of these three forays, he cited my book, *St. Croix 1493: An Encounter of Two Worlds* (1995), on the same subject and has taken issue with my conclusions concerning a Salt River landing. In my book, I critically examined the long-accepted account of the event by British scholar Samuel E. Morison and concluded that, in spite of some missteps, he was fundamentally on target with his findings. My attorney friend has been so active of late disseminating his revisionist ideas with no one about the scene to oppose or criticize them that I have recently felt compelled to take up my pen and at least present my original conclusions in order to give the public a choice. In so doing, I was somewhat surprised to discover that I could have originally analyzed the available sources more thoroughly and in greater detail and offered a stronger conclusion in that first book. It

Representation of the Santa Maria.

took my friend's gentle prodding to move me to reconsider the matter and undertake a more thorough analysis, which I offer here. For that opportunity, I am in his debt.

The major contours of the generally accepted story of the Columbus "landing" on Saint Croix are well known. On his second voyage from Spain to the West Indies, commenced at Cádiz on September 2, 1493, Columbus, with his fleet of seventeen ships, set sail across the Atlantic, stopping for two days, October 5–7, at the island of La Gomera in the Canary Islands and then completing the crossing to the West Indies in twenty-one days. On November 3, the fleet entered Caribbean waters at the island of Dominica. Because that island lacked safe anchorages on its eastern coast, however, the ships continued on a northerly course to Guadeloupe, where they made a stop and picked up several Taíno Indians, who, apparently, were being held captive there by Caribs. On

REVISITING THE COLUMBUS LANDING ON ST. CROIX

November 10, the fleet departed Guadeloupe and continued in a west northwesterly direction, passing a number of small islands along the way, some of which the Admiral named—Montserrat, Redonda, Antigua, St. Christopher, etc. On November 14, sailing in that same direction toward the North Virgin Islands, the mariners saw an island on the horizon that the Indians on board identified as "Ayay," or Hàhi-hai, according to Père Raymond Breton. [Breton 1665] Columbus judged that the island was large enough and attractive enough to merit a stop in the hope of finding some Indians with whom he might "have talk." He made a brief stop there and renamed the island Santa Cruz, according to the eyewitness sources.

Arriving at a "harbor" located, I believe, along the island's northern coast, sixteen ships of the fleet stood off, or hove-to, while the Admiral's flagship moved in closer to the entrance of the harbor. From there, he had a longboat launched with some twenty to thirty men aboard to reconnoiter a settlement of a half dozen or so huts located that they saw along the shore. That settlement was very likely on the western side of the bay, where considerable archaeological remains have subsequently been found.

From there the mariners proceeded inland a short distance through a heavily forested valley, guided by some of their Indian passengers. Finding no Indians along the way, they returned to the harbor after a short time and began to row back to the waiting vessel just offshore. En route, they encountered an Indian canoa (canoe) rowed from the west by Caribs; on board were several apparent Taíno captives who had been recently castrated as the result of having been taken prisoners in a raid. Initially astounded by the sight of the fleet, the Caribs on board the canoa then made a dash toward the safety of the harbor, but they were cut off and rammed by the Spanish boat. A brief skirmish ensued, in which several Indians were killed and several others taken as prisoners. One Spaniard suffered an arrow wound and died several days later. Several of the Caribes were taken on board the anchored ship as captives. Then, just six or seven hours after his arrival and after having named the island, Columbus directed the Spanish ships to set a course for the islands that lay visible on the northern horizon, the Virgin Islands. From there, he then proceeded on his way to Española. Such is the general outline of the encounter of 1493 at St. Croix.

That event was described as they saw it by three eyewitnesses in the Spanish fleet. In addition, a number of other writers, who either interviewed eyewitnesses or read some of original writings of eyewitnesses, have left useful written accounts as well. A brief glimpse at those individuals and their respective backgrounds at this point might prove helpful in evaluating the relative merits of their observations, some of which are quoted in my narrative that follows. For purposes of organization, the narrators of the 1493 visit to St. Croix can be arranged into three categories, namely eyewitness, secondary, and derivative accounts.

The eyewitness accounts were composed by three individuals who were present with the Spanish ships on that day. Dr. Diego Álvarez Chanca most likely viewed the events of the landing and encounter from the deck of the Admiral's flagship and from that vantage point penned his "La Carta que escribió a la ciudad de Sevilla, Febrero a Marzo 1494." Second, Michele de Cuneo was the young adventurer who commanded the longboat that Columbus dispatched ashore in order to find natives with whom he might "have talk." Cuneo described those proceedings in his "Lettera" (15–28 Octubre, 1495, Savona, Italy). And third and last was Guillermo Coma, whose "Lettera" appeared in Nicolo Scillacio's *De Insulis Meridiani atque Indici Maris Nuper Inventis*, published in Pavia on December 13, 1494. With their own eyes, these three men all viewed what transpired on that day, and each has left us a vivid descriptive account.

The second group consists of four secondary accounts, composed by persons who had direct access to the eyewitnesses themselves or to the writings of eyewitnesses. First among them were the short narratives of Simone dal Verde and Giovanni de Bardi, both Italian merchants who were residents of Spain at that time and who had direct contact with the sailors and Indians when they returned from the 1493 voyage. Both of these accounts were published in Guglielmo Berchet's *Fonti Italiane per la Storia della Scoperta del Nuovo Mondo*, published in 1893. The third of these secondary accounts was the biography of Columbus, written by his son Fernando Columbus, *Historia del Almirante*. Finally, there was the voluminous work, *Historia de las Indias*, written by the remarkable ecclesiastic Bartolomé de las Casas.

Of lesser importance were the descriptions written by Andrés Bernaldez, Antonio de Herrera y Tordesillas, Peter Martyr, Alonso de Santa Cruz, and Hernán Pérez de Oliva. In one manner or another, none of these writings was firsthand but all were derived from the authors listed directly above. The original texts of all of these accounts—eyewitness, secondary and derivative—can be found with side-by-side, facing-page English translations in my book *St. Croix 1493: An Encounter of Two Worlds*, and they are referenced as such.

OVERVIEW OF GEIGEL'S CLAIMS

Geigel argues in his lectures and in his book that Columbus sailed along the southern coasts of the islands lying to the west of Guadeloupe and that this trajectory determined his sailing course as he approached St. Croix, that is, to the south of the island. This one idea determines the entire substance of his theory. According to Geigel, the Admiral held his course along the south side of St. Croix and made his landing on November 14, 1493, either on the southwestern shore of the island just east of Sandy Point, or on the western shore of the island somewhere to the north of Sandy Point, instead of at the Salt River estuary on the northern coast as has been assumed for some time.

In support of this conclusion, Geigel proposes the following evidence. First, he argues that an approach to Ayay along the north shore would have been improbable due to the "extremely shallow water" in that area. Second, he asserts that an anchorage at Salt River would have been impossible due to extreme wind and sea conditions. He notes that the prevailing winds, from the east and southeast, as he understands them, would have made a landing on the north shore difficult at best while those same conditions would have been propitious to a southern or western landing. Third, he maintains that the cultivated fields and other evidence of Indian settlements that were observed from onboard the approaching fleet were in fact located along the southern, not the northern, coast. In support of this contention, he cites the existence of some thirteen Indian settlements along the southern section of the island and eight on the west end. And fourth and finally, he maintains that the west end of the island offered better anchorages as manifested in the presence there of excellent holding ground there and by implication a better opportunity to go ashore and have talk with the natives. The following text is dedicated to a critical examination of each one of these points in Attorney Geigel's argument.

GEIGEL'S SOUTHERN THEORY

It should first be recalled that Columbus, with the experience of his first voyage already behind him, was not sailing completely in the dark. His navigational strategy for the second voyage focused on an approach to the Indies from the east at a more southerly latitude than his first voyage. His purpose was to visit some of the islands that had been mentioned to him by the Indians of Española during his first visit, namely *Matinino, Isla Caribe,* and possibly others as yet unknown to him. He was aware that, according to the information received from the Indians, those places would lie to the east and perhaps south of Española. That he entered the Caribbean archipelago at Dominica is a direct result of that awareness. That navigational strategy therefore meant that the Leeward Islands would lie to his north, more or less along the arc of his proposed route back to Española. If he were to visit those islands, indeed even pass by them, he would necessarily do so from the south. It follows clearly that such an approach was not the result of some grand sailing strategy but followed from the simple facts of navigation and geography, namely his approach was from the south. In other words, Columbus was not tied to visiting islands on the south side in any theoretical sense, and this was certainly the case relative to his call at St. Croix.

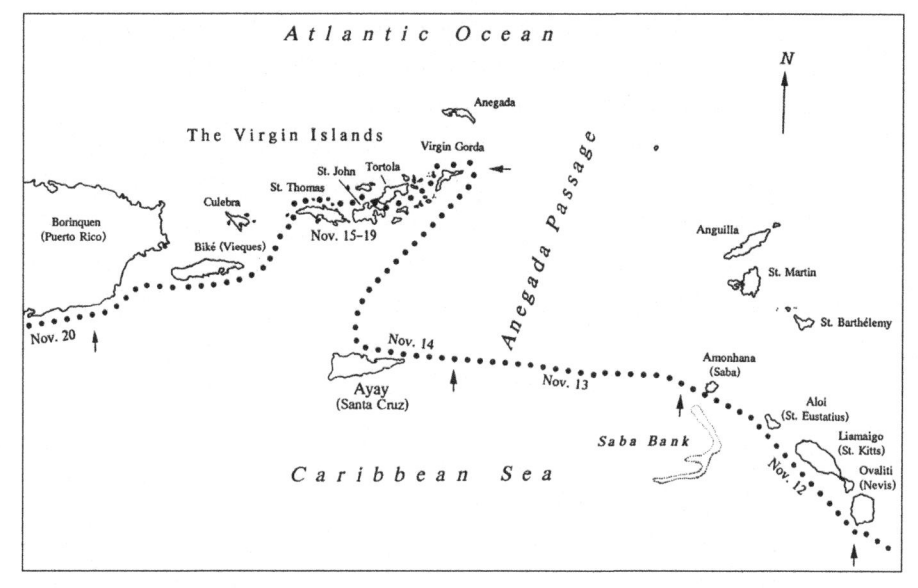

Map showing the sailing route of the Spanish Fleet in 1493.

THE NORTH SIDE OF ST. CROIX

If the fleet did not approach St. Croix from the south, what is the evidence, if any, that it did so then from the north? First, from the testimony of the eyewitness accounts, it is clear that the fleet was following a course from Guadeloupe that would take it through the Virgin Islands. Dr. Chanca makes this point perfectly clear when he writes that the islands to the north, which were eventually visited, "lay on the course that we were taking" (*que estaba en el camino que habiamos de facer*). [Highfield 80] It is certain therefore beyond a reasonable doubt that the fleet approached the Virgin Islands archipelago in the direction of those northern islands and was as a result already on a course well to the north of St. Croix, a fact that would have made a south side approach and landing highly unlikely.

As the ships approached the archipelago and the islands came into view, the Indians onboard who were quite familiar with the islands of the area would not have failed to identify the Virgins to the north and

SEA GRAPES AND KENNIPS

Ayay (St. Croix) lying some forty-five or so miles to the south. In passing, it has been suggested by some scholars that the island in question may have been mistakenly confused for St. Martin from the very start. This, however, is unlikely for several reasons. In the first place, the name Ayay was used for this large island from the start, and it was moreover identified with the present St. Croix. Second, this same name, spelled slightly differently as *Hàhi-hai*, is clearly identified with Santa Cruz by Père Raymond Breton some 150 years later in his well-known dictionary. [Breton 1665] Third, there are no valleys on St. Martin of the kind described by Simone dal Varde. And fourth, it would have been impossible to see the Virgin Islands by the naked eye from St. Martin, as is witnessed in the narrative of Dr. Chanca. The suggestion of a St. Croix-St. Martin confusion can therefore be readily dismissed.

Ayay clearly referred to St. Croix and its location was doubtlessly pointed out to the Spaniards for the first time by the Indian passengers onboard ship. At that point, any navigator worth his salt would have chosen to make a call at this, the largest and most impressive of any island in the group. Following this reasoning, the fleet would have naturally stopped along its northern coast in order to maximize exploration options, that is to say, the ships could call at St. Croix and at the same time retain the option of afterwards visiting the islands to the north as well. Since there were no islands visible to the south side of St. Croix and since the Indians on board were fully aware that no such islands indeed even existed, a passage on that side, that is, the south side, offered no attraction and no advantage that is readily apparent from the present perspective. This interpretation is supported by the fact that after his short stay at St. Croix, Columbus did in fact sail north to the Virgins, informed and guided by his Indian passengers.

APPROACH TO THE ISLAND

Geigel opposes a northern approach to St. Croix for another reason as well. He argues that the waters along the island's north shore and through the Buck Island Channel were narrow and "extremely shallow."

REVISITING THE COLUMBUS LANDING ON ST. CROIX

He suggests that those conditions would have inhibited Columbus from sailing that route. In fact, that channel is about one and three quarters of a mile wide at the narrowest point, with average depths of no less than thirty feet and, in most places, a good deal more. The seventeen ships of the size and draught of those in Columbus's fleet would have passed with no difficulty through that channel. But being the cautious mariner that he was, Columbus might well have sent one or two of his smaller vessels through the channel while directing the remainder of the fleet to sail further offshore, to the north of and around Buck Island. However it may have been in reality, Columbus had that choice open to him. There is absolutely no reason to think, however, that he was prevented from sailing the north shore because of the so-called "navigational hazards" proposed by Geigel. Indeed, coasting near shore was the Admiral's common practice as was his preference when he later sailed through the North Virgins; there is no basis for assuming that he did not follow that same practice along the north coast of St. Croix.

ANOTHER SITE ON THE NORTH SHORE?

The points raised in the immediately foregoing discussion, in the absence of hitherto unknown documentation, make the probability in favor of a landing on St. Croix's north shore rather pronounced. But was it necessarily at Salt River? Might it have been that the fleet actually stopped at some other point along St. Croix's north shore? The geography and the physical features of that stretch of coast argue against such an interpretation. First, the entire north shore of the island is enclosed from the very east end of the island all the way to Judith's Fancy, with only several, small inconsequential breaks, by an extensive, fringing reef system. Assuming that the three or so openings that now punctuate that reef existed at that time, it remains a likely conjecture that they were extremely narrow, then as now, presenting little opportunity for safe entry and anchorage by vessels of any size. But the overriding consideration at this point in the discussion should be the presence of the Indians aboard ship who would have in all likelihood directed the newcomers "seeking talk" to the political and economic and certainly the cultural center of the island, namely to the extensive Indian settlements at Salt River, the area they referred to as Ayay.

A CULTIVATED ISLAND

The documents suggest that the Spanish ships not only sailed west along the north coast but moreover that they were relatively close to shore, as they could clearly see the details of the gardens and settlements. As the fleet coasted west, the men on board were offered a panoramic view of the island, which enabled them to describe clearly the cultivated fields that they saw on land. Michele de Cuneo observed that the island was "most beautiful and fruitful" (*bellissima et frugifera*). [Highfield 84] And Andrés Bernáldez added: "Another day at mealtime, they arrived at an island that had a very good appearance and was very populated." [Highfield 112] It was also described by Simone dal Verde as having "a beautiful valley that was very well cultivated." [Highfield 90] To these descriptions should be added the words of Alonso de Santa Cruz, who wrote some thirty years later that: "It used to be very populated, having twenty villages and more Indians." [Alonso de Santa Cruz 2:500–02]

What was the location of this developed, well cultivated part of the island? It has long been a well-known archaeological fact that settlements and villages were lacking on St. Croix's extreme southern and western coasts in the final ceramic period, and certainly just before the European intrusion. [See Vescelius; Tilden] This was in large measure due to the dearth of year-round streams and fresh water in that part of the island, then as is the case still today. The village at Fair Plain, located perhaps a mile inland from the sea and not immediately visible from aboard ship, was the only exception to this rule. Otherwise the island's southern and western parts—certainly the stretch from Long Point Bay to Sandy Point referred to by Geigel—were lacking in settlements as would have been evidenced by major archaeological remains. It is not at all likely then that Dr. Chanca was referring to the south side of the island when he wrote: ". . . Another day at mealtime, we arrived at an island. It appeared very good to us because it appeared to be well populated as witnessed by the many cultivated fields that it had." (*Parecia muy poblada, segun las muchas labranzas que en ella habia.*) [Highfield 80] There can be little doubt that this passage, as well as the preceding ones, refers to a location on the north shore of St. Croix where the vegetation and streams that flow there, then as today, contrast sharply with the aridity of the extreme southwestern shore.

THE INDIANS ON BOARD THE SHIP

When he arrived in the Caribbean, Columbus was already aware of the general direction of Española, as well as the fact that there were islands lying between him and that destination. He had with him some five Taíno Indians from his first visit to Española in 1492, who had been taken to Spain and then returned to the Caribbean on his second voyage. In addition, Columbus also picked up some Taíno Indians during his landfall several days earlier in Guadeloupe, who, by their own testimony, were captives of the Caribs. Most likely they came originally from islands to the west. They earned their rescue and passage home on the basis of their ability to act as guides and interpreters for the Spaniards. And what is equally clear is that they had some knowledge of the geography and people of the area, including the name and location of Ayay, subsequently named Santa Cruz (St. Croix) by the Admiral. In addition, they told Columbus in advance that the people on Ayay were Caribs, they guided a group of Spaniards ashore through a valley on that same island, and they later informed them that St. Thomas was uninhabited.

Would the Taínos have advised the Spaniards to call at St. Croix? In the first place, the island is the largest in the area of the Virgin group and on the perimeter of the Vieques Sound. It measures some eighty-two square miles in size as opposed to twenty-seven for St. Thomas and nineteen for St. John. In addition, it is relatively flat and long and would have presented a much more attractive and inviting profile on the horizon than the other islands. Guillermo Coma writes: "As it was attractive in its appearance and inviting to the seamen, it was decided to make port there." [Highfield 88] Archaeological evidence indicates, moreover, that it had a far greater population than the other two islands at that time. In fact, the Indian women told them that those latter islands were uninhabited. If the Spaniards wished to contact people and engage in talk, would it not have been highly probable that the captive Taínos would have directed them to St. Croix?

That raises yet another question. How would the Taíno interpreters have described St. Croix to the Admiral and where would they most probably have directed him to sail if he had made it clear to them that he wished "to have talk" with the people there? If archaeological records are to be trusted, Salt River was clearly the center of the island's population and culture at that time, due to the estuary's central location, the fertile soil in the surrounding area, the existence of fresh water, and the abundant riverine, estuarine, and marine resources. Indeed the importance of Salt River for the island's pre-history cannot be underestimated. Its location at center island on the north coast gave it a central location facing north to the Virgin Islands and west to the Vieques Sound bordering Puerto Rico, Vieques, and Culebra. The estuary at Salt River was by every indication the optimum aboriginal settlement on the southern arm of the Vieques Sound.

This contention is supported by the presence of the island's most extensive and impressive archaeological remains, among which stood, on that estuary's western shore, the island's only ceremonial ball-court, or *batey*, in fact the only one of its kind to the east of Boriquen (Puerto Rico). [Hatt 1924] There were, in addition, ceremonial plazas that were lined with ritual, free-standing petroglyphs of considerable size, the only ones ever discovered on the island. It is certain that this was the center of Taíno settlement and culture in times past and that, moreover, it would have continued as the center of things under Carib domination. It is reasonable then to assume that Columbus's Indian passengers directed him to the estuary on the north shore for the simple reason that there lay the recognized center of things and there dwelled the people with whom Columbus would desire to "have talk."

REVISITING THE COLUMBUS LANDING ON ST. CROIX
MOTIVE FOR LANDING: "TOMAR LENGUA"

It has been sometimes said by some writers that the Spanish fleet desired to take on water and such was its principal motive for stopping at St. Croix. Moreover, those same observers have also held that the Salt River estuary was for the most part brackish and that better sources of fresh water could have been found along the southern and western coasts. The fact of the matter is that none of the eyewitness sources mentions any such need to "take on water." The fleet had just stopped at Guadeloupe four days earlier and after having spent some twenty days in the trans-Atlantic passage, it is certain that the fleet filled its casks from that island's abundant sources of sweet water.

In fact, one of the seamen remarks on the high quality and abundance of Guadeloupe's water. Simone dal Verde observes that: "Upon asking the captain about the quality of the waters, he told me that having stopped at the first island of the Chanballi (Guadeloupe) and having thirst, he came upon a streamlet of clear, beautiful water, from which he drank." [Highfield 97]. Fresh water being plentiful on that island, there would have been no need to fill the casks again just four days after that visit. Moreover, a brief six to seven hour layover on Ayay would have allowed insufficient time for the men from seventeen ships to load their casks on lighters, go ashore, find a good source of water, fill their casks, and then return to their ships. Nor could any idea of replenishing the water of seventeen ships been entertained while sixteen of them were hove-to well off-shore. The search for drinking water was therefore not a concern for the visiting Spanish vessels.

All of the eyewitness sources are quite clear about the Admiral's principal motives for stopping at Ayay. Chanca writes: "Then the Admiral ordered a boat of men to go ashore and talk [with the people] if possible to learn who they were. We also had need of information concerning our course." [Highfield 81] To that observation he adds: "Although the Admiral had never sailed this course, he was proceeding along the correct route as it turned out. But because doubtful matters should always be investigated with the greatest possible scrutiny, he wished to speak

SEA GRAPES AND KENNIPS

[with someone] there." To these comments, Coma adds: "Since laurels and also bramble bush appeared in the distance, a small exploratory boat was launched in order to learn something of the language, customs and ways of the islanders." [Highfield 88] The Admiral's objectives then in stopping at Ayay were quite clear. He wished to talk with the natives, find out exactly who they were, learn something of their customs and ways, and, last, confirm his course to Española to the west. To accomplish this objective it was not in any way likely that he would have stopped at a minor island or visited a recess area on one of the larger islands.

LANDING LOCATION

Having established that Columbus and his fleet approached St. Croix along its north coast, it remains to determine actually where he put his men ashore. Cuneo says unequivocally that: "We sailed to a beautiful bay." [Highfield 85] Several of the texts say that the ships sought to "tomar porto," or make a landing at a harbor, or a partially enclosed coastal area. Coma has this to say: "As it was attractive in its appearance and inviting to the seamen, it was decided to make port there." [Highfield 89] And Chanca adds : "We sailed there and made port along the coast." [Highfield 81] On this point, all of the eyewitness sources are indubitably clear—that the point of landing was a port, or a harbor.

Three locations along St. Croix's north coast qualify today as harbors, or ports—Tague Bay on the east end, Christiansted harbor, just to the the west of there, and Salt River at mid-island. Of these three, Tague Bay is completely enclosed by a long fringing reef and had only scant Indian settlement. Christiansted harbor was also enclosed by a long fringing reef but had a small but dangerous opening toward one end; it also had a sizable Indian settlement. Both these locations lacked, however, the fertile, cultivated valley described below by Simone dal Verde. Finally, the Salt River estuary was also enclosed by a reef, but with a small opening at its center. More importantly, the mouth of the estuary funneled into a long, fertile valley, which was in effect the settlement

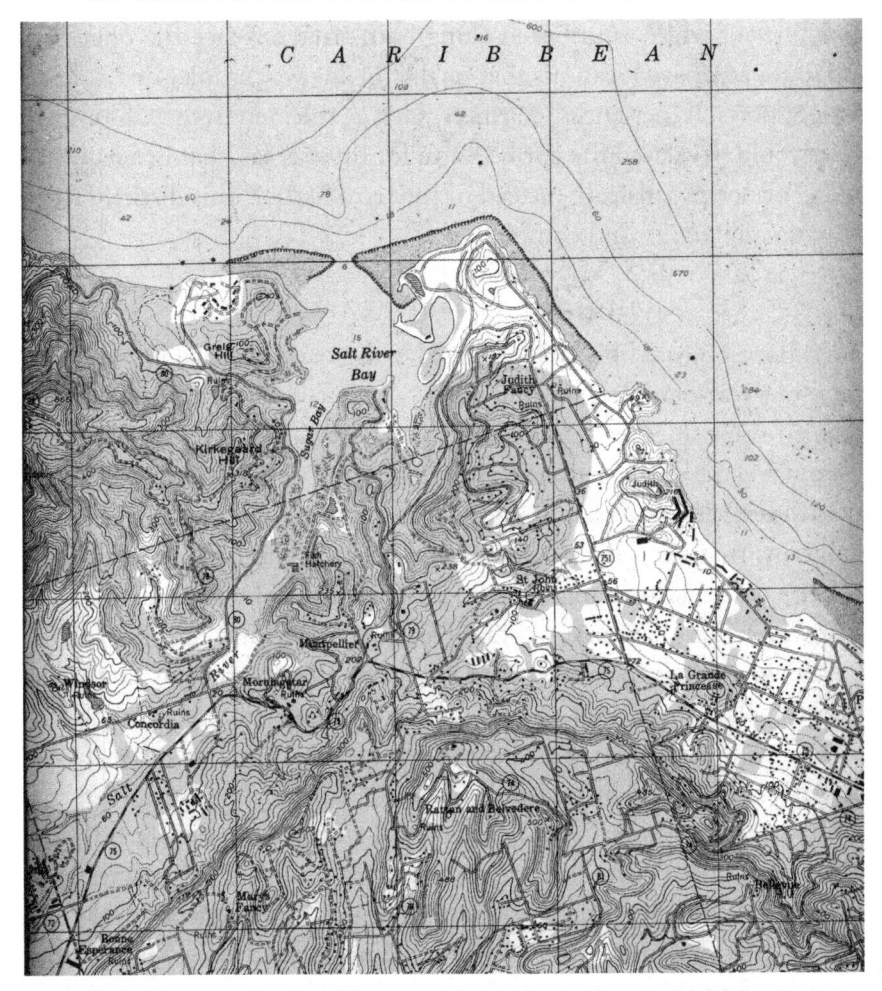

Salt River estuary as shown on the U.S. Geological Map of Christiansted, 1958.

center of the island. Taking all these features into account, Salt River best fits the descriptions given by the eyewitness accounts.

In sharp contrast, neither the south shore near Sandy Point nor anywhere along the west end of the island as cited by Geigel qualifies as a "porto," or a "harbor." Both of those coasts are characterized by long, unindented shorelines, with no bays, no estuaries, no arms of land extending into the sea, and no enclosing, fringing reefs. The straight shorelines of white sand beach along both stretches face the open sea and in no way have locations that qualify in any way as inlets, bays, harbors, or ports. Experienced mariners, such as the men in the Columbus fleet, would have used the correct term for those areas, that is, a leeward "rada," or open roadstead, instead of the term harbor. This distinction is clear, unambiguous, and compelling.

ANCHORAGE VERSUS HEAVING-TO

It has been objected by Geigel that the approach and the entrance to the estuary at Salt River would have been too difficult for any of the Spanish ships to enter safely for even a short visit. Moreover, the area just outside the entrance to the estuary certainly is not an ideal location to anchor a sailing vessel of any size, and indeed not a small fleet. He maintains that the calcite bottom, strewn with coral heads and rocks would have been too dangerous for an anchorage of any kind. The fact is, however, that that same location has always been and continues to be a place where sailing craft anchor regularly. The presence of hundreds of lost anchors that litter the sea bottom at that location testifies not only that the anchorage was difficult but, at the same time, that it was regularly undertaken by intrepid seamen.

On a fine, sunny day in March of 2006, I engaged in a debate with my friend Attorney Wilfredo Geigel on the Columbus landing question, sponsored by the National Park Service of the Virgin Islands and held at the newly acquired event center building located on a hill directly above the Salt River estuary facing east. Standing on a balcony of that building, the thirty or so attendees were afforded an excellent view directly down on the estuary entrance, the reef and the harbor. Clearly visible underwater was the narrow shelf—perhaps some 150 yards in all—just outside the reef in about fifteen fathoms of water. Riding at anchor there were three sailing vessels, one of them some thirty feet in length; the other two were smaller. The point of this little discursion is to point out that sailing vessels can and do anchor in that location without imminent danger. The boats lay on their anchor lines in an

REVISITING THE COLUMBUS LANDING ON ST. CROIX

east-west alignment, without any threat of being thrown onto the reef. That sunny day provided a striking example of the very point that I later made in the debate.

Nowhere, however, has the claim been made, either in the sources or in my writing, that all seventeen of the Spanish ships actually entered the bay or anchored outside at that location. The sources say that one vessel did anchor, presumably the flagship, and moreover those same sources give an important clue concerning the disposition of the other sixteen ships. Cuneo notes, for example, that the maneuver of heaving-to by the Spanish vessels was a common practice, and that was exactly what the fleet did. "When we did not anchor, we kept the ships hove–to in order that we would not make headway and that for fear of running aground in these islands." [Highfield 85] This maneuver of heaving-to—setting the sails to starboard and lashing the tiller to port in order to force the craft to head up into the wind and thereby greatly reduce way. This lying-to, or *pairo* in Spanish, as the outcome of this maneuver is called, was a common practice during the voyage, especially in the passage through the numerous Virgins. In this manner all but one of the ships in the fleet were able to spend some "six or seven hours" at the island without dropping anchors.

One other critical point should be made here. Geigel posits that the entire fleet sailed to the west end of the island, the leeward side, where anchorage would have been safe and easy. If this were indeed the case, why would the majority of the vessels have found it necessary to heave-to in the first place as the sources clearly indicate, when they could have easily dropped anchors onto sandy bottoms in clear, relatively shallow water of the west end? That heaving-to maneuver, however, would have been necessary only if the fleet had made a stop at Salt River where conditions for an anchorage were problematic that day in light of the heavy seas.

THE DIRECTION AND FORCE OF THE WIND

Geigel argues that the winds at that time would have constituted an impediment to any anchorage at Salt River, either at the entrance to or inside the estuary, stating that "according to the coastal pilot when the northern winds are blowing, which is normal in November, the ground swells accompanying these winds are especially heavy in the vicinity of White Horse [Rock]." [Geigel 25] But just a few pages later, we are told that, according to the expert witness Iván Guzmán, a contemporary seaman who works the waters around St. Croix, that "On the average day, the trade winds that blow from the east-southeast are from 10 to 15 knots." [Geigel 26] Using this contradictory information concerning seasonal wind directions, Geigel proceeds to argue that such winds would have been favorable to a southern landing but unfavorable to a northern one. A quick glance at a map shows that exactly the opposite is true. Any wind blowing south of east raises the swell on the south shore and throws a heavy surf onto the beaches in areas such as the Long Point, where there is no protecting reef.

Such easterly winds would have had the effect of causing a vessel anchored before the Salt River estuary to lie in a westerly or northwesterly alignment on its anchor, that is, parallel to the reef and not under threat of being thrown upon it, just as those ships were lying on the day of the debate. The northern winds that Geigel refers to mistakenly are locally called the "Christmas winds" and normally begin to blow heavily from the north or east of north in mid- to late December as a result of cooler air from North America moving high pressure zones into the northern Caribbean Sea region. In any event, those varieties of winds would neither have prevented an anchorage just outside the Salt River estuary nor heaving-to further out to sea, in particular for a limited period of time.

And finally, if the prevailing winds did in fact come from the east and northeast as Geigel maintains, then the waters off the west shore of St. Croix, that is, on the leeward side, would have lain calm, as is usually the case today. If the Spanish fleet had ended up there under those circumstances, I repeat, why would there have been any need for the vessels to heave-to as the sources imply they actually did?

REVISITING THE COLUMBUS LANDING ON ST. CROIX

THE LOCATION OF THE INDIAN VILLAGE

According to the Spanish accounts, the seamen who went ashore encountered a small Indian village on the shore very close to the sea. This distinction is quite important, for, as we know from archaeological sources, there were few if any settlements exactly on the shore on the southwest corner of Ayay in that period. At Salt River bay, the village was located precisely on the shore. Most prominent among these narratives that support just such a location are the words of Coma who writes: "As he headed for that part of the harbor where six huts could be seen . . ." [Highfield 89] Bernáldez likewise supports the proximity of the village to the point of landing when he writes: "Certain of the men jumped from the said boat onto land and went to a village where the people had already fled into hiding." [Highfield 112] Writing some years later, the Spanish "cosmographer," Alonso de Santa Cruz wrote that Spaniards approaching the same location encountered "found 4 dogs on the shore." [Alsonso de Santa Cruz 2:500-02].

It is important here not to lose sight of the fact that these accounts square exactly with the archaeological evidence relative to the settlement at Salt River. Gary Vescelius and other archaeologists have demonstrated abundantly that the remains of the Indian habitation there was located precisely on the beach and not at some point further inland. [Vescelius 1952] Salt River is the one settlement in existence at that time which matches this description perfectly. It is equally important to reiterate the fact that there were no such beach-side villages directly on the shore on the south side of the island.

THE FERTILE VALLEY

Simone dal Verde was an Italian merchant living in Spain who interviewed members of the twelve ships' crews of the second voyage—the Captain Antonio Torres, the Master of one of the caravels and a Pilot—after their return to Spain in April of 1494, as well as some dozen Indians who returned with those same vessels. Those interviews provide interesting testimony that is lacking in some of the eyewitness sources.

SEA GRAPES AND KENNIPS

Verde writes that the Spaniards who landed in the longboat "were guided through a very great density of trees of about 3 miles, and after climbing a hill, they saw a beautiful valley that was very well cultivated." [Highfield 96] This passage describes perfectly the Salt River valley that extends inland from the mouth of the estuary for several miles, covered, then as now, by dense forest. The hills that form the valley rise to an elevation of some 400 feet on the western side and 300 feet on the eastern. At a distance of several miles inland, the seamen who made the trek obviously climbed the sides of the hills and were given a view of the well-watered valley that they were following. They described it as highly fertile with lush vegetation on all sides and native dwellings that had been abandoned as they approached. The important point here is to note that not only does this description fit the Salt River valley perfectly in a geographical sense but moreover that it is the only such location that exists anywhere on St. Croix.

What "beautiful valley" might have been located on the south shore or on the western end of the island, both of which are completely flat? The south shore, in addition, is particularly arid with neither dense forest nor well-cultivated fields. Nor does the archaeological record show Indian settlements or artifacts of the kind and quantity implied by Verde's narrative. Indeed, it seems patently clear that this reference to a densely forested valley points to the Salt River estuary that extends inland to the south for several miles, but it has been furthermore well established in the archaeological record that the same valley was inhabited and cultivated during all phases of pre-Columbian St. Croix, along an area extending all the way into present-day Estate Glynn.

ELEMENTS OF THE ENCOUNTER WITH INDIANS

All the sources recognize and describe contact with an Indian canoa just as the Spanish longboat was returning to its mother ship after a short visit onshore. A close examination of the descriptions of that encounter yields significant insights concerning the actual location of the event. Chanca writes: "Just as this boat intended to return to the ships with the

Indians in a canoa similar to the one in the encounter at Salt River in November 1493.

prisoners that had been taken, from downwind along the coast came a canoa in which there were four men, two women and a boy." (*Ya que esta barca se queria tornar á los navíos con su presa que habia fecho por parte debajo por la costa venia una canoa en que venian cuatro hombres é dos mugeres é un mochacho.*) [Highfield 81] Evidence from the Bardi letter also supports the approach of the canoa along the coast toward the Spanish ships, though the numbers of individuals aboard was seen as different: "Skirting the shore, they caught sight of a boat with 8 Canabali, 5 men and 4 women." [Highfield 98–101]

The expression "from downwind" clearly means "from the west," a fact deduced from the direction of the prevailing winds as well as from Columbus's navigation to that point in the voyage. In addition, the

SEA GRAPES AND KENNIPS

phrase *por la costa*, "along the coast," can only refer to the north coast of the island. But what are the reasons to conclude that the coast referred to could only have been the northern coast and not the southern or western end of the island, as Geigel suggests? Had the location of the encounter been at the west end of the island, the canoa could indeed have approached from the west but directly from the open sea and not possibly "along the coast," as the description clearly states and as anyone familiar with the geography of the island certainly knows. Similarly, if the canoa had approached the south shore, it would have rounded Sandy Point directly from the open sea and immediately encountered the Spanish ships had they been there. There would have been no coast to approach along. The sense of these texts manifestly establishes the location of this event on the north side of the island.

THE APPROACH OF THE INDIAN CANOA

It has been established that the Indian canoa approached St. Croix from the west. There is every reason to believe that it was returning from Puerto Rico or Vieques to the west of St. Croix, inasmuch as the craft had on board a captured Taíno who had been recently castrated, as was the Carib practice when raiding their enemies. The vessel rounded the extreme northwestern tip of St. Croix and made its way eastward to the Salt River Estuary, hugging the shore as it proceeded. Between that northwestern point of St. Croix and the next bluff of land (Baron Bluff), which lies 5.8 miles to the east, the northern shore between those two points is markedly concave in configuration. At the most southerly point of the concavity the shore lies about 5,300 feet to the south of a horizontal line between the aforementioned points. The Indians in the canoa moving along the coast would therefore not have caught their first sight of the fleet until just after rounding the point referred to by the sources. This scenario matches perfectly with the geographical outlay of the area around Baron Bluff. Furthermore, one of sources notes that the canoa, after rounding that bluff, came to a halt some "two Lombard shots" from the fleet, or some 1,800 feet of distance, as the Caribs stared on in amazement at the Spanish vessels, the likes of which they had never before seen. This description also squares exactly with the assumed position of Columbus's ship at anchor just outside the estuary, as well as with the events of the conflict that followed, including the direction and location of the refuge that the Indians sought among some shallows lying near the reef.

SHOALS, ROCKS, REEFS, OR SHALLOWS IN THE SEA

The account of the skirmish between Caribs and Spaniards at Salt River is well known and need not be recounted in any great detail here. Nearly all the sources take notice of the fact that after the Spaniards had rammed and sunk the returning canoa, the "Camballi," who found themselves overboard swimming for their lives, were able to secure footing on some shoals or shallows in the open sea. There are only several possibilities for the location of those shoals and reefs in the general proximity to the entrance to the estuary. [See The U.S. Geological Map]

First, White Horse Rock is located about 400 yards off Salt River Point just to the east of the entrance to the estuary and has been pointed to by some authorities and subsequent historians as the likely location of the refuge. However, White Horse was not at all the probable place referred to in the accounts because its location to the east of the estuary does not take appropriate account of the approach of the Carib canoa from the west. Besides, that outcropping is usually heavily awash by even moderate seas and would have been an extremely difficult refuge for swimmers in an open sea. A much more likely location was the natural shallows, or shoals, lying quite near to shore, just off the reef to the west of the entrance to the estuary at Salt River. [The U.S. Geological map] Moreover, this is exactly the direction that the Caribs would have taken in their attempt to escape from their pursuers using the closest trajectory to land. The U.S. Geological Map shows these shoals quite clearly. This same map, however, shows no such rocks or shoals on the island's west side between Hamm's Bluff and Sandy Point. It is obvious therefore that the incident described in the eyewitness accounts could not have taken place off the southern and western shores of the island, but the geographical features of the Salt River area show, once again, a near perfect match with the information contained in the narrative sources.

ISLANDS VISIBLE TO THE EYE TO THE NORTH

If the preceding were not evidence enough in support of a Salt River landing, then there remains the following. Eyewitness sources relate that after six or seven hours at St. Croix, the fleet departed toward land that could be "seen by the [naked] eye." All things considered, that land could only have been the Virgin Islands lying to the north. There were simply no other islands within view. Later that same day, Chanca remarks that "Afterwards that same day we departed the island, not having been there more than six or seven hours. We sailed for some other land which appeared to the eye to be on the course that we were to follow." (*Luego aquel día partimos de esta isla, que no estariamos allí mas de seis ó siete horas, fuemos para otra tierra que pareció á ojo que estaba en el camino que habiamos de facer.*) [Highfield 82–83] Not individually named, these islands were St. Thomas, St. John, Virgin Gorda, and a host of other, smaller islands. What is absolutely self-evident to anyone who is even minimally familiar with the locations in question is that while those same islands can be seen quite clearly with the naked eye from the northern shore of St. Croix, including the estuary at Salt River, it is and would have been altogether impossible to see them from any point along St. Croix's south shore and highly problematic from the west end. On the basis of this piece of evidence alone, a landing at that south shore location must necessarily be ruled out as simply inconsistent with the physical facts.

AYAY: WHAT'S IN A NAME?

Several of the early visitors and writers were very clear in stating that the Taíno name for St. Croix was Ayay. Peter Martyr writes that "they chaunced upon an other muche bygger than any of the reste, which the inhabitans caule *Ay Ay,"* [Highfield 107] Similarly, Alonso de Santa Cruz makes note that "the Indians called it Ayay and according to others it was called Cibuqueira." [Alonso de Santa Cruz 2:500–02]

The Arawakan word *Ay* may well throw meaning on the original Indian designation for Ayay. The Agabama River and the River Ay, an estuary, are both attested in Cuba. The Río de Ay rises in the mountains of Tuerto in Cuba and then flows south to the coast, emptying into the Caribbean Sea, forming an estuary to the east of the town of Casilda. In a personal communication, the archaeologist Alfredo E. Figueredo has drawn my attention to the reduplication of this word in the name Ayay, which may here possibly mean literally "water, water," or something similar, in reference to an estuary that runs into the sea, that is to say, a place where fresh water meets sea water. If this conjecture proves to have any validity—and caution must be drawn that it will require additional research before a more positive evaluation can be made—then that interpretation would lend considerable weight to the location of the so-called Columbus landing at Salt River.

SUMMARY

No single piece of the evidence discussed here in itself alone presents an absolutely ironclad case for the Salt River estuary as the site of the Columbus landing. However, the composite documentation when considered in a close analysis with the physical feature and geography of the island makes a most convincing argument. In fact, it would not be overly bold to maintain that it is difficult indeed to make an effective argument for any other location on the island. I am confident therefore in positing that my brief examination of Attorney Geigel's claims in contrast with a close examination of the texts themselves has established the following points as compelling and convincing.

Let us note first that the navigational course followed by the Spanish fleet upon leaving Guadeloupe was to the north of St. Croix, with the intention of returning by dead reckoning to Española by way of The Virgins and Puerto Rico. As he approached the island from the east, the Admiral evidently decided to visit St. Croix, the largest and most attractive island in sight, to talk with the natives in order to determine who they were and to gather information on his location and the direction of his course. Approaching the island on a northwesterly course, it is therefore geographically highly probable that he made land along the island's north shore. The cultivated fields and associated populated settlements referred to in the narratives are confirmed in the archaeological record as being overwhelmingly on the northern side of the island at that point in time.

Moreover, if Columbus wanted to have a talk with the natives, the Indians who served as his interpreters and guides on board his ship would most likely have directed him to the Salt River bay area, which was the most heavily populated, the best known, and the most important cultural center of the island. This is attested by the presence of a *batey* (ball court) and ceremonial plazas, both lined with the only freestanding petroglyphs of any size ever found on the island. The landing site was identified by the seamen onboard by the word "porto," that is, a port or harbor, in Spanish, an enclosed, protected area along the shoreline, in which ships could find safety and anchorage from the dangers of the open sea. Nothing in the west and southwest parts of the island qualifies for this designation to the degree as does the Salt River estuary. On the contrary, the western shore of St. Croix constitutes nearly seven miles of completely open roadstead (Sp. *rada*), with no feature resembling a port or harbor.

Approaching that porto, only one ship actually anchored at that site and that was on the narrow underwater shelf just outside the estuary at Salt River. The other vessels hove-to as was the general practice in open seas during that voyage. This action closely adheres to the restrictions imposed by geographical features and marine conditions present at that location. At the same time, there clearly would have been no need for "heaving-to" on the western end of the island, inasmuch as that protected, leeward location ordinarily has moderate winds and smooth seas. The Indian settlements at Salt River were located inside the estuary, close by the shore and not inland, as attested by several of the eyewitness sources. By Geigel's own admission, there were no major settlements on the shore in the southwestern area.

The densely wooded, fertile valley, as described by Verde, clearly points to the Salt River valley, surrounded on both sides by hills of at least three to four hundred feet. Both the south shore and the western end of St. Croix are entirely flat with no valley at all like the one described by Verde.

During the violent encounter between Caribs and Spaniards, the Carib canoa approached the estuary from the west along St. Croix's northern coast, catching sight of the Spanish fleet only after rounding what the sources called a point, which can now be identified as Baron Bluff; no such geographic features exist on the southern or western sides of St. Croix.

Just before departing the island, the Spaniards report being able to see land by the naked eye (*tierra que pareció a ojo*). The fact is that those same islands can seen almost daily to the north from Salt River, but they are impossible to ever see from the south shore of St. Croix, and only rarely possible and only at certain parts of the west end.

Finally, there is emerging linguistic evidence that the name Ayay, which may very well describe a place where "water meets water," applies to Salt River and not to anywhere on the south shore. Taken collectively and analytically, this combined evidence argues overwhelmingly in favor of a Salt River estuary landing by the Spanish fleet and completely discredits a south shore or west end one.

CONCLUSIONS

It seems to me that, in view of the preceding analysis undertaken independently of any inquiries of others, the probability of a north shore landing at Salt River by Columbus and his fleet on November 14, 1493, is relatively strong whereas the probability of such a landing on the southern or western shores of the island is sharply limited. Pending the discovery of some further documentation or the unearthing of compelling archaeological evidence to the contrary, I will stand against Attorney Geigel's South and West Shore thesis in favor of the North Shore interpretation, that is, at Salt River, as argued above. At the same time, I remain sincerely indebted to my good friend for raising the question again and providing the occasion for revisiting the issue.

REFERENCES

Berchet, Guglielmo. *Fonti Italiane per la Storia della Scoperta del Nuovo Mondo.*

Breton, Père Raymond. *Dictionnaire Caraïbe-François*, réimprimé par Jules Platzmann, édition facsimilé, Leipzig, 1665.

Breton, Père Raymond. *Dictionnaire François-Caraïbe*, réimprimé par Jules Platzmann, édition facsimilé, Leipzig, 1666.

Las Casas, Bartolomé de. *Historia de las Indias*, México: Fondo de Cultura Económica, 1951.

Christiansted, V.I. (17064—F6–TF–024). *The U.S. Geological Survey.* 3 panels. Scale: 2:24,000. 1958. (Photorevised 1982)

Colón, Fernando. *Historia del Almirante.* Madrid, 1892.

Geigel, Wilfredo A. "Salt River in St. Croix: Columbus Landing Site?" Paper presented at a Conference at the University of the Virgin Islands, St. Croix campus, November 12, 2000.

Geigel, Wilfredo A. *Salt River in St. Croix: Columbus Landing Site?* Puerto Rico: El Libro Inc., 2005. 43 pp. Ill., maps.

Hatt, Gudmund. "Fra Vestindien." *Nær og Fjærn* (Feb. 1924), pp.103–19. Ill., map.

Highfield, Arnold R. *St. Croix 1493: An Encounter of Two Worlds.* St. Thomas: Virgin Islands Humanities Council, 1995. 8+ 159 pp.

Santa Cruz, Alonso de. *Islario General de Todas las Islas del Mundo.* Con un prólogo de D. Antonio Blázquez. Madrid: Publicaciones de la Real Sociedad Geográfica, 1918–1920. 2 v.

Vescelius, Gary Stockton. "The Cultural Chronology of St. Croix." An Essay submitted to the Faculty of Yale College in partial fulfillment of the requirements for the degree of Bachelor of Arts as a Scholar of the House. New Haven: Yale University, 1952. 106 pp.

The city of Ramallah, near Jerusalem.

CHAPTER 26

THE PALESTINIANS OF ST. CROIX

ZUHDI ABDALLAH'S department store on the corner of Company Street and King Cross Street in Christiansted today stands empty and desolate. In the late 1950's, Zuhdi was one of the first Palestinians to come to St. Croix to open a business and start a new life. It seems like only yesterday that, in 1962, I met him and purchased my first guayabera shirt from his wares. A lot of water has passed under the bridge since that time. That first Palestinian store has now closed, but it has left behind a trail of Arab-owned clothing stores, gasoline stations, grocery stores, supermarkets, and, yes, shopping centers to the Palestinians' incredible tales of success on St. Croix.

Other Palestinians also arrived in St. Croix in the late 1950s, and in the early 1960s. Some of those early arrivals could be seen pushing wheeled suitcases along the streets of Christiansted. They would park them on a corner and then open them wide to the delight of a gaggle of eager female customers. To their startled eyes would appear a mini-department store, replete with dresses, blouses, shoes, jewelry, household items, and a little bit of just about everything. It was a marketing strategy that had immediate appeal.

In an amazingly short period of time, I would see the same vendor, selling fruits and vegetables from the trunk of an old car under the shade of a tree on some busy corner. From there it was just a jump away for them to owning a small store of some kind. This was the rapid trajectory taken by many of the first Palestinians who came to St. Croix.

One such street vendor was Fathi Yusuf, who pulled up stakes from the West Bank city of Ramallah and struck out for St. Croix to make a new life for himself. And make a new life he did! His rise through the commercial ranks of our island has been nothing short of phenomenal. Today he and several of his five sons own and manage the hugely successful Plaza Extra Supermarkets on both St. Croix and St. Thomas. In addition, he has helped a number of his relatives from Ramallah also gain a toehold and advance themselves here, including his well-known nephews Ali, Solomon, and Yusef, the owners of the Food Town Market in Princesse. Fathi's amazing success has proven to be a strong attraction for the many who followed him here.

The majority of these folk are called Arabs by local Crucians and that is not incorrect, as nearly all of the newcomers speak Levantine Arabic and are Muslims. A rough estimate would place their numbers at approximately 1,300 on St. Croix and perhaps 600 on St. Thomas. Some 90 percent of them trace their origins to the city of Ramallah and its surrounding small towns and villages on the West Bank. With a population of some 25,000 souls, Ramallah is located about six miles north of Jerusalem and today serves as the administrative center of the Palestinian National Authority. Their giant leap from the West Bank to St. Croix has been the result of a long, confused chain of events that has dominated political life there over the past century.

Palestine was created from the British Mandate in 1920 from a territory within the Ottoman Empire, which collapsed at the end of World War I. Turkish domination of Palestinian Arab people had endured for more than 400 years, from 1516 to 1918. The Allied Western victors of that war carved protectorates out of the collapsed empire, which resulted in seemingly endless colonial conflicts that spanned the remainder of the 20th century. Out of that struggle, the various states of the Near East, The Gulf and The Magreb—Morocco, Tunisia, Libya, Egypt, Lebanon, Syria, Iraq, Iran, Saudi Arabia, Kuwait, Qatar, Bahrain, Yemen, and the Gulf States—all emerged, though none without conflict and strife.

Palestine felt the greatest impact from these developments largely because at that same time the Jews who had survived the European Holocaust sought to return to their ancient homeland—from their perspective Israel, not Palestine—just as the war ended and as the Arab struggle for independence was at its height.

The declaration of the Jewish state of Israel carved from the heart of Palestine in 1948 quickly deteriorated into a bitter struggle between Palestinian Arabs and newly arrived European Jews, one that still rages to this day. The Jews, fleeing from a history of ghettoes, pogroms, and death camps of Europe after World War II on a burst of energy supplied by Zionism, won the opening encounters of the fight, driving tens of thousands of Palestinians into exile in refugee camps in neighboring states such as Syria, Lebanon, Libya, Kuwait and others. During the period from 1948 until 1967, the West Bank, including Ramallah, fell under the control of Jordan. During that time, emigration from those parts was quite heavy.

The 1940s and the 1950s became a period of heavy immigration from Palestine and Israel to numerous parts of the world, including Latin America and the Caribbean. Zuhdi Abdullah mentioned above was one of the first to arrive in St. Croix. I have been told that one of his uncles preceded him to the Virgin Islands by several years landing on St. Thomas. In a short time, Abdullah established a clothing store at the corner of Company St. and King Cross St. in Christiansted. It was soon a success, becoming a permanent fixture of the town. His brother Ahmed and his sons later set up a grocery store in Princesse. Zuhdi raised and educated his sons, and when grown and educated, they set up their own businesses on St. Thomas. This scenario represents a fairly accurate picture of the manner in which the immigrants arrived and the manner in which they established their own families and new businesses. Successes such as these attracted others in the homeland to follow.

How was it that the newcomers succeeded so naturally and quickly? There are two important responses to this question. The first response deals with conditions on St. Croix at the time of their arrival. From the beginning of the American period in the Virgin Islands in 1917, Crucians were stymied from entering business, in short due to the reluctance of banks to extend them loans. They were therefore little able to amass the capital required to set up and develop businesses, and such ventures moreover came to be regarded as the domain of outsiders, who had access to capital and know-how. The resulting vacuum and the concomitant growing demands of the public were filled initially by immigrants from Puerto Rico, Vieques, and Culebra beginning in the 1920s. Very small Hispanic grocery stores popped up everywhere. When the first Palestinians arrived forty years later, there existed therefore little serious competition and much room for growth and expansion.

In the second place, the Palestinians generally relied on the family model to operate their businesses. In a recent conversation with the brothers Khalid and Solomon Ali, the owners of Food Town, they expressed the idea that it was the strong role of Palestinian fathers and the cohesiveness of the family under them that account for the success they have achieved. Having an authoritative and respected leader over an effective chain of commend made all the difference.

The typical Palestinian businessman also worked closely with his uncles, brothers, cousins, nephews, and sons. The extended family unit under the aegis of Arab patriarch enabled the new entrepreneurs to work together in relative trust and cooperation toward sharply defined goals. When the time was appropriate, they might expand the initial business by opening another store under another family member. Or they might venture into an entirely new undertaking. In a relatively short period of time, they set up gas stations, convenience stores, clothing stores, and hardware stores. It was a formula that worked well.

Maintaining ties with the homeland has proved to be another important key to success. Although it is difficult—indeed impossible for some—to travel to Israel, St. Croix's Palestinians have held onto continuities of language, religion, and culture with the West Bank. In this manner, they have remained connected with their parents and relatives, provided them with sustenance and support, arranged marriages for their children, and often encouraged their countrymen to travel to St. Croix. When newcomers arrive, they can count on a helping hand

THE PALESTINIANS OF ST. CROIX

from those who were already established. Herein lies the power of the homeland connection. Not surprisingly, St. Croix is a well-known name in Ramallah.

Nothing resembling a localized Palestinian community or Palestinian section has ever developed here. Rather they live scattered over different parts of the island. The construction of their dwellings is generally heavy and solid, almost as if they were expecting an assault, perhaps a recollection of life on the West Bank. But it is also an indication that they have come to stay. Perhaps more important, the dwellings are generally large, built to accommodate big families and multi-generational residency and lifestyle.

A sense of community has been achieved in another manner as well. In the 1970s, they established a Mosque in the Catherine's Rest area, called Abu Bakr after the first Companion of the Prophet Mohammed. Interestingly enough, it is peaceably located right beside the Jewish Synagogue. It has been served since the 1970s by Imams who have hailed from various parts of the Muslim world. The present Imam is Abu Mosab, a Palestinian. Consequently, some 200 to 300 believers are able to gather each week for Friday prayers, followed by social interaction.

Many local Arabs agree that their religion and their strong belief in God have played a major role in their advancement. But some of them quickly acknowledge at the same time that the environment here makes it easy for them to become less religious than they once were and that their children have become not only less religious but less Arab as well. That is a natural result of the latter being born and living in a secular society such as ours and, of course, it poses a problem for those among them who are acutely aware of the need to retain their cultural and religious identity in this foreign land now and into the future. That need will grow more acute as the third and fourth generations soon arrive.

So there has appeared a pressing need to do something now. Most Arab children attend private schools where their peers are local and North American, thereby exposing them to the worlds of cell phones,

SEA GRAPES AND KENNIPS

texting, popular music, extreme media influences, foreign behaviors and mores, and the like. In response to this, the Arab patriarchs have established a school where their children will be exposed to the Arabic language, history, and worldview over which they have some control.

The future is always difficult to envision, as well as one's place in it. So it is for the Arab community along with everyone else. But what is certain is that when children grow up in an entirely new environment and culture, with a new language, foreign peers, and new way of life, they inevitably part company to one degree or another with their parents, and in the doing, something is lost at the same time as innovation is being added.

So it will most certainly be the case with our Virgin Islands Palestinians. The strong need to succeed, the inexhaustible work ethic, and the previous connections with the homeland and the past that marked the psychology of the first generation all lose their tensile strength as they are replaced by other perspectives, other values, other needs, other desires that arise in their children but which remain alien to the parents. Ramallah is a long ways distant, generations pass like ships in the night, and the world is ever-changing. Palestinians here will have to come to grips with the reality that loss of identity may ultimately be the dark reverse side of the bright coin of success.

Anna Elizabeth Heegaard

CHAPTER 27

CRUCIAN DANES & THE FAMILY OF CHARLOTTE AMALIE BERNARD

THIS PAST MONTH, a group of twenty-one Danes visited our islands for two weeks. One and all they were in search of Crucian ancestors from the Danish West Indies dating back to the eighteenth century. There was nothing new about this visit insofar as over the years hundreds of Danes have come to this island in search of ancestors. What made this group special was that their ancestors were people of color.

The leader of the group was Jens Benoni Willumsem, a mild-mannered, thoughtful Dane from the island of Funen. I had the pleasure to sit down with him and his charming wife Kirsten for lunch several weeks ago at the Sand Castle Beach Club, looking out over an incredibly blue sea as we talked. The attractions of our island for our Danish friends is unmistakable. Jens had already come to the islands a number of times previously in his quest for information about his connections to his Crucian past and family. On this day, Jens laid his story before me, and it was indeed fascinating.

In 1968, he visited the islands as a young man for the first time, taking part in the semi-centennial celebrations of the transfer of the islands from Denmark to the United States. Two years later he returned as an exchange student and studied Virgin Islands history under noted historian Dr. Marilyn Krigger at the then College of the Virgin Islands in St. Thomas. She opened the past up to the young Dane through reading, travel, and meeting a wide variety of locals. Jens knew that he was related to Anna Heegaard and other Crucians, but he was not certain about all the particulars. Some forty-odd years later, by the time of our meeting, he had put together many of the details, had written a short account of the story, and had a captivating tale to tell.

The story of Jens Willumsen and the Crucian Danes begins over two hundred years ago in the mid-eighteenth century. After Denmark purchased St. Croix from France in 1734, the island was placed squarely on a course of sugar production, based on the division of the island into over three hundred plantations and on the introduction of thousands of Africans as enslaved workers.

At the outset, the development of sugar production was intended simply to make money. But as with most human endeavors, it also generated unintended consequences. Among a number of such unforeseen outcomes, the sexual attraction of European men for the enslaved African women was one. It immediately produced children of mixed race. Borrowing from the Iberian terminology, the Danes called those children "Mulattoes," that is, having one African parent and one European.

Within one short generation, the Europeans, finding these first female people of color attractive, eagerly took them as mistresses, concubines, and mates if not as wives in relatively open relationships. The children of these unions of one White and one "Mulatto," now having one grandparent as Black and three White, were called "Quadroons," or "Mustices."

As the Quadroon females among them were considered to be very comely, they were quickly embraced by the next generation of Europeans as mates, sometimes as recognized mothers of their children and sometimes as common law wives. This new generation of people of color, since they had one African grandparent out of eight, the other seven being European, were called "Octoroons." Now the racial distance was far less between them and the Europeans. The Willumsen family and a number of others in Denmark, proudly trace their origins back to this mixture and its nomenclature.

At the very beginning of this family's line of descent stands Charlotte Amalie Bernard, born on St. Croix in 1753 as a slave. She was most

THE FAMILY OF CHARLOTTE AMALIE BERNARD

probably what was then called a "Sambo," that is, a person who was one-fourth White and three-fourths Black. When Charlotte Amalie was twenty-one, she was impregnated by her master, plantation owner Lucas Uytendahl, or possibly by one of his sons; she gave birth to a daughter, Susanna, in 1774. The mother and daughter, both slaves, lived at the Uytendahl residence at One King Street in Christiansted. When Lucas died in 1786, he gave Susanna both his name and her freedom.

Charlotte Amalie in 1777 bore another daughter, one Lucia Assenius. The father was Erich Assenius, a merchant seaman, who was ten years older than Charlotte. At that time, 1776, Assenius was the Captain of a Danish ship called the "Ada," which had just brought a shipload of captives from West Africa to St. Croix under his command. During his stay on St. Croix, he met Charlotte and left her with child. She delivered Lucia the following year. The infant received her father's name, was soon baptized, and began her life at the Uytendahl residence on King Street, Christiansted in the care of her mother and sister Susanna.

Records reveal that after Lucas Uytendahl's death in 1786, Charlotte Amalie and her daughter Lucia were owned by Judge Advocate General Ludvig Eigtved. In 1793, he fled to Tortola because of embezzlement charges, and Charlotte Amalie and her daughter were offered for sale at a public auction in Christiansted. Charlotte Amalie was purchased for 200 rigsdalers by Hans Cappel, who was living with Susanna at that time, but the sale of Lucia was postponed due to uncertainty about her ownership.

When Lucia attained the age of seventeen in 1794, she was offered for sale at auction; the highest bid of 400 rigsdalers came from her mother and sister, and they became her new owners. However, as her mother and sister did not have all the money needed for the purchase, they had to raise a loan from the Royal Treasury with security in the form of Lucia herself. Finally the following year, when the loan was paid back, Lucia received her *Fribrev* (letter of freedom), and she became a free person of color. Charlotte Amalie and her daughters were obviously making their way in the world.

SEA GRAPES AND KENNIPS

At the age of nineteen, Lucia herself gave birth to a son, Peter Andreas C. Petersen. Two years later she brought another son into the world, one Hans Peter Wilhelm Petersen. The father of the two boys was Thomas Petersen, a Danish ship-owner and merchant who lived on St. Croix. Although Thomas shortly thereafter married a White woman, with whom he had a third son Christian Boas Petersen, an ancestor of the Armstrong family that owns Bülowsminde today, he did not abandon his family with Lucia. After his marriage, he presented his sons with a sum of money and a property at #47 Hill Street, Christiansted, on which stood two houses. Jens Benoni Willumsen has made it very clear that from this young Quadroon woman and her two sons has flowed the Crucian source of his family in Denmark.

As a free woman of color, Susanna followed her mother's inclination and entered into liaisons with European men from quite an early age; together three such encounters produced four children. The first of these occurred in the late 1780s, when she met the Dane Jakob Heegaard, born in 1761, who later became a Treasurer in the Customs Department in Christiansted. That relationship produced a daughter, Anna Elizabeth Heegaard in 1790, when Susanna was scarcely sixteen.

The second relationship was with a ship captain and mariner, Hans Cappel, born 1752. Together they engendered two daughters, the first by the name of Christiana, who was born in 1793. A second daughter, Sophia Cappel, was born to the union in 1796.

The fourth and final child resulted from Susanna's encounter with Peter A. Wittrog, a merchant who was born in 1771. That union produced a son in 1803, one Johannes Wittrog, who later became a butcher and a respected plantation owner. It was in this manner that the struggle of a Quadroon woman up from slavery, resulted in the advance of her four Octoroon children to the status of free, respected people of color.

It should be remembered that since the fathers of all these children were White Europeans and that the mother was a West Indian Quadroon, the children were therefore all Octoroons. Physically, this meant that they were all very light-skinned in complexion and predominantly

THE FAMILY OF CHARLOTTE AMALIE BERNARD

European in physical features. This creation of an intermediate group between the island's Whites and Blacks became and remains a key to understanding race relations in the Danish islands. Envied and imitated by the Black population and both feared and admired by the Whites, the Quadroons, Octoroons and beyond, were all caught squarely between the two groups, enjoying the advantage of slight privilege and at the same time suffering the disadvantage of continuing discrimination and bias. Theirs was a conundrum that produced great anxiety and no few mixed emotions.

Anna Heegaard was and remains by far the best known member of this family both here and in Denmark, though ironically she produced no direct family line of her own. Born in 1790, she was the first of Susanna's children. She grew up in her mother's house under the care and tutelage of both her grandmother Charlotte Amalie and her mother Susanna. Doubtlessly, she spent long hours in her mother's cloth and knitwear shop in town, learning about business and money. Obviously, she adopted many of her mother's attitudes and ways toward life, money, and men.

At the tender age of nineteen, Anna took up residence with a certain Christopher Hansen, a lawyer. Later, in 1815, she became the "housekeeper" for an Irish merchant, Paul Twigg, who had recently acquired the house on King Street where Anna had lived with her mother and grandmother. In 1821, she entered a relationship with Captain H. C. Knudsen, who owned a plantation and served as a colonial adjutant. Together they first lived on estate La Grande Princesse which he administered and then later moved to his Estate Belvedere on the island's north side. It is to be noted that for eighteen years Anna shared bed and board with three men of notoriety, wealth, and substance in Crucian society. During that time, she rose from the daughter of an ex-slave to a position of some means and status in Danish colonial society. She was determined to rise even higher. That final step was made possible when she met Peter von Scholten.

In 1804, at the age of twenty, Peter von Scholten arrived in St. Thomas

SEA GRAPES AND KENNIPS

Peter von Scholten

with the rank of Ensign , and twenty-three years later, in 1827, he became interim Governor-general for all the Danish islands in the West Indies. Eight years later, he was named full Governor-general. He was an intelligent, handsome man with seemingly endless ambition. At about the same time that he assumed this new role, he formed a lasting relationship with Anna Heegaard. Unfortunately we know little about the particulars. But it seemed to be a match made with ambition and wealth in mind, along with an element of conscience thrown in for good measure. The relationship flourished until von Scholten departed St. Croix for the last time in 1848.

It has been claimed by some that Anna's imprint apparently marks a number of important actions that Peter undertook as Governor–general, including the Organization and reform of the Free-colored class (1832); the improvement of conditions among the slaves (1834); the School Ordinance of 1839; and finally Emancipatin itself (1848). Von

THE FAMILY OF CHARLOTTE AMALIE BERNARD

Bülowsminde

Scholten believed in Emancipation but at the same time was convinced that it should come gradually, in cadence with the proper preparation for the trials that freedom would entail. The presence of Anna can be felt at his elbow at every step, for was she herself not after all a member of the Free-colored class and had not her grandmother, Charlotte Amalie, and her mother, Susanna, both been ex-slaves, who were still alive and with her at that time? With the influence of her considerable means and her constant presence at the Governor-general's side, how could she not have exerted a force on Peter's thinking and actions?

Together they obtained land in 1834 and created Bülowsminde, a fine country house located on a hill overlooking Christiansted just to the west of town. It was named for Frantz Christopher Bülow, Denmark's Adjutant General to King Frederik VI, under whom von Scholten served as an assistant earlier in his career. But even at that level, the stigma of color managed to influence their lives. Though they lived and entertained in the big house, they still felt constrained to build a smaller house for Anna, called Hafensight, where it might be seen by all that the "Lady of Color" maintained a residence apart from that of the Governor. In time the entire property came to be owned solely by Anna after Peter's departure in 1848, devolving at her death in 1859 on her family heirs.

Peter von Scholten died in 1854 in Altona and was interred in the stately Assistens Cemetery in Copenhagen. Now alone, Anna rented the large residence at Bülowsminde to the new governor, H.D.F. Feddersen (1851–55) and after him to the lawyer H. R. Arnesen for several years. She lived the rest of her life at Hafensight, surrounded by her servants and with frequent visits from her relatives. The estate provided them all with a generous lifestyle, what with the country-side's abundance of food—fruits, vegetables, fowl, and small livestock. Her life devolved into a routine. Every Monday, Nanan, as she was called, boarded her carriage and made the short trip to Christiansted, passing estates Beeston Hill, Merman Hill and Contentment along the way, there to look after business, to deliver a part of her estate's bounty to her family, and to visit with friends and relatives.

When Anna Heegaard passed from this life on January 1, 1859, at the age of sixty-nine years, she left a will and testament that reveal the extent of her holdings and her generosity. To her two nieces, Mrs. Susan Eliza Knudsen and Mrs. Agnes Petersen, daughters of her sister Lucia, she left Bülowsminde and the bulk of her possessions, including some money and jewelry. To Kammeraad Hans Peter Wilhelm Petersen, Royal Treasurer on St. Croix and son of her aunt Lucia, she bestowed her carriage and two horses. And to twenty-two various relatives and friends she bequeathed $4,950.00 in individual sums of fifty, one, two, three, and four hundred dollars apiece. She requested burial at Estate Aldersville, the property of her half-brother Johannes Wittrog.

Anna Heegaard's moment in the sun was brief and fleeting. During the fifty years following her death, her family on St. Croix all but disappeared. The few surviving relatives either lacked the will or the

THE FAMILY OF CHARLOTTE AMALIE BERNARD

wherewithal to maintain the estate, and it quickly went to weed and seed. On April 3, 1888, the Colonial Treasurer on St. Croix auctioned Bülowsminde and Havensight (Numbers 6B, 7A, 6C, 7B, 13B, and 35B) for the sum of $114.88 for the non-payment of taxes. At that time, the plantation was valued at only $3,822.00. It was purchased by Robert Armstrong, whose descendents still own the property today.

That decline might be explained in part by the fact that some members of Charlotte Amalie's descendents left St. Croix for Denmark during the nineteenth century. Most prominent among these came from the line of Christina Cappel, daughter of Susanna by Hans Cappel, a merchant seaman, already referred to above. Cappel went down in a shipwreck off the coast of Norway in 1798, leaving his property in Christiansted to his daughters of color. As a member of the Free-colored class, Christina could not legally marry a White man, but she did enter into a common law marriage with a Scottish merchant, James Miller of St. Thomas, a plantation owner. Among their several children she bore him was Agnes Patterson Miller, who later married H.P.W. Petersen. The two of them became the great-great-grandparents of our visitor Jens Benoni Willumsen. That process of the transition to Denmark was set in motion, when, in 1848, one of her sons, Benoni James Petersen, at ten years of age, was sent to Copenhagen for his schooling.

Benoni never turned back. He received a degree in medicine, opened a clinic, and later became the head of a hospital in the town of Naskov in southern Denmark. His marriage to a Danish woman produced three children, one of whom became the grandmother of Jens Benoni Willumsen and a whole host of young Danes today. It is in the lives of those people that the family of Charlotte Amalie—who by the way, lived to the ripe old age of 103—made the transition from the Danish West Indies to Denmark. How remarkable it is that the Danish descendants of Charlotte Amalie, born a slave in the eighteenth century, have managed to hold onto that thread of family and maintain intimate contact with the people and land of their origin over these past 150 years. Their tenacity is nothing short of remarkable.

SEA GRAPES AND KENNIPS

As the Virgin Islands completes a full century of post-colonialism after the sale of the islands by Denmark to the United States in 1917, the remaining connections between the likes of Jens Benoni Willumsen and his clan, and the islands whence his family sprang suggest that what we should be commemorating and perpetuating on "Transfer Day" and in the coming centennial events of 2017, is our mutual Virgin Islands-Danish Heritage in all of its many facets. These Danish Crucian folks are living proof that the connections between our two societies are not only historical, economic, and political but also biological and familial, and, yes, they run very deep.

The Saint Louis docked in Havana harbor, June 1939

CHAPTER 28

THE VIRGIN ISLANDS AND THE VOYAGE OF THE DOOMED

IT MIGHT COME AS A SURPRISE to many Crucians to learn that their small island became involved in an international controversy with Germany, the United States, Cuba, and a number of other nations at the outset of World War Two.

On May 13, 1939, the German ship the *Saint Louis* slipped anchor and sailed out into the North Atlantic from the port of Hamburg en route to the Caribbean island of Cuba. On board were some 937 passengers, all but seven of them very anxious Jewish refugees. They had very good reason to be worried.

The rabidly anti-Semitic Adolph Hitler had some five years previously taken the first step toward seizing power in Germany with his famous *Ermächtigungsgesetz*, or Enabling Act (March 23, 1933). His intense hatred of Jews and his desire to rid Germany of their presence became a harsh reality on the nights of November 9 and 10, 1938, during the infamous *Kristallnacht* actions. On those two savage nights, Nazi henchmen employed brutal aggression against the Hebrew community, physically attacking them and destroying their homes and their property. In a very short time, the death camps would become a stark terror. While some Jews slumbered in the face of the grave threat, others decided then and there that it was time to take action.

It was under these circumstances that the ship *Saint Louis* under the command of a German Captain, Gustav Schröder, set sail on a voyage to Cuba. Its mission was to deliver a boatload of Jews to a destination that would accept them as refugees. The expectations of those passengers must have been a good deal less than sanguine what with the Nazi

SEA GRAPES AND KENNIPS

Gustav Schröder, Captain of the Saint Louis

flag flying on the bridge of the vessel and a portrait of Der Führer hanging in the dining hall. After two weeks at sea, the vessel made port at Havana on May 27, 1938, only to learn that one week previously 40,000 Cubans had demonstrated against their arrival. And moreover, the Cuban government was so locked in controversy about admitting so many Jews that the process became completely stalled.

On June 2, Capt. Gustav Schröder sailed the *Saint Louis* out of Havana harbor with its destination Miami. For two days the vessel steamed slowly back and forth along the Florida coast near Miami, seeking permission to land. After that was consistently denied, Schröder considered running his ship aground on the beach to force a landing in the face of American government resistance. Rebuffed by the United States, on June 6, the *Saint Louis* laid a course back to Havana but en route turned north and headed back to Europe. A return to Germany meant sure death in concentration camps for all of the Jews on board.

Feverish negotiations enabled most of the passengers to be accepted as refugees in other nations instead of being returned to Germany, thereby saving many lives. Great Britain agreed to disembark 287 en route. The voyage ended in Antwerp, Belgium (June 17), where, of the remaining 619 passengers that were allowed to disembark there, some 224 were accepted by France, 214 by Belgium, and 118 by The Netherlands. Scholars have estimated, however, that in the final analysis some 254 of the passengers ultimately wound up in Nazi death camps and perished after those assisting nations were conquered by Germany.

The voyage of the *Saint Louis* became a desperate symbol of the plight of European refugees and in particular of Jews, caught in the jaws of the Nazi state. In the case of the United States, the President and State Department turned their backs on the victims, fearing that any loosening of immigration controls might result in a wave of unwanted immigrants. Some smaller nations, however, acted more nobly. The Dominican Republic, as one example, offered to accept 200,000 refugees. Our own Territory of the Virgin Islands passed a resolution opening its doors to the many who were in distress. Haiti also showed itself to be open to such acceptance. Just why their offers were not acted upon remains still a mystery today.

One need not search overlong to understand the willingness of our small islands to lend a hand to threatened Jews. In fact, they had never been strangers in Denmark nor in the Danish West Indies. Both Sephardic and Ashkenazi Jews were present in Danish lands from the middle of the seventeenth century. In 1719, they were allowed to have a synagogue in the Danish town of Fredericia. Toward the end of the eighteenth century, Denmark entered a period of reform inspired by the European Enlightenment, which affected all strata of Danish society, including the Jews. Slowly, Jews gained access to high schools and to craft guilds and were soon allowed to purchase land, to erect synagogues and serve in the military. With time, the universities and medical schools opened up to them. The final stroke came in 1814 when full civil rights and citizenship were extended to all Jews, permitting them to assimilate fully into Danish society.

Repercussions of these events were of course felt in the Danish colonies in the West Indies. By the mid-eighteenth century there were small Jewish communities on both St. Croix and St. Thomas, and they played important roles in the economy. In the 1730s, a certain Jew by the name of Seeberg created a silver coinage that served the entire community. By 1764, a modest synagogue appeared in St. Croix and in 1796 a larger one in St. Thomas. Although they were forbidden to purchase land, Jewish merchants did establish homes and warehouses in the towns from which they operated their businesses. It is important to note that they established contacts with Jewish communities in other parts of the Caribbean—Curaçao, Panama, and the like—which facilitated trade and promoted prosperity for the entire community. By the time the United States purchased the Danish islands, Jews had been rubbing shoulders with other Virgin Islanders for the better part of two centuries.

And so Virgin Islanders acted almost instinctively on November 18, 1938, when, after the barbarism of the Kristallnacht, the Legislature of the Virgin Islands resolved that "when and if existing barriers are removed that they [Jews] shall find surcease from misfortune in the Virgin Islands of the United States." Those "barriers" were the ones that had already been erected by the Unites States government earlier in 1938. Our Virgin Islands legislators were anything but timid for in that same resolution they directed that "copies of the resolution be sent directly to the President, the Secretary of State, the Secretary of Labor, the Secretary of Interior, and to members of the Press." An article in the November 21, 1938, edition of the *Virgin Islands Daily News* said that the "expression of the sentiment of the people of the Virgin Islands on the persecution of Jews in Europe was passed unanimously." The men

Virgin Islands Governor Lawrence W. Cramer (1935–1940) seen to the far right

who served on the 1938–1940 legislative council were: Joseph Alexander, Ralph de Chabert, Halvor Berg, Fredrick D. Dorsch, Isaac Boynes, Christian Joseph, David C. Canegata, Paul E. Joseph, and Cornelius Penthany.

The U.S. government's reaction to the V.I. offer was immediate. The Department of State sent a letter to all authorities calling this action, "incompatible with existing law." The Attorney-General refused to render an opinion. Virgin Islands Governor Lawrence W. Cramer (Aug. 23, 1935–Dec. 14, 1940), taken aback by the response, signed an executive order on November 2, 1940, as a follow-up to the Legislature's resolution, whereby 2,000 refugee families were to be admitted into the Virgin Islands immediately. The idea behind this plan was to provide a sanctuary, or a place of waiting in the Virgin Islands, for those Jews who had been promised visas, thereby removing them from the immediate threat of German aggression.

But the American government continued to stimy the plan, claiming that the influx of foreigners might be used by the Germans as cover for the introduction of spies into the U.S. Thousands of Jews were therefore trapped inside the S.S. death machine, while the German propaganda at the same time made the most of America's awkward response to the situation. If the United States did not want to admit them to their country, how could anyone criticize Germany for its policies, the propaganda machine blared? In one last effort, many Jews made pathetic, unanswered appeals for help to escape. Acting V.I. Governor Robert M. Lovett (1940–1941) remarked: "I have been overwhelmed by correspondence of a most poignant nature."

One such plea arrived from the pen of Gerhard Neumann who wrote on Feb. 14, 1941, from the Camp de Gurs, a notoriously squalid holding area for the deportation of Jews from France to the concentration camps of Germany and Poland. Neumann wrote to Governor Lovett: "We should be very much obliged to you, if you could improve our actual situation by giving us permission to stay in your territory till we can immigrate to U.S.A. We are aware, that we do an extraordinary step in applying to you. But that is our last chance." Acting V.I. Governor Lovett responded to the desperate man's "last chance" by responding that: "I regret to inform you that a procedure for giving effect to the plan affording temporary refuge in the islands has not been worked out by the State Department and the Department of the Interior."

In this doomed danse macabre, the Virgin Islands Legislature and the Governor acted with extraordinary courage and moral conviction. Those long-forgotten actions were finally recognized on September 18, 2011, by the presentation of a special award by the David S. Wyman Institute to the People of the Virgin Islands through their representative Congresswoman Donna Christensen at the Fordham University School of Law. On that occasion, Dr. Rafael Medoff, Director of the Institute, recognized the courage of the Lilliputian V.I. Territory in defying far greater powers, having the following to say: "At a time when most of the world turned the other way, the leaders of the Virgin Islands extended a brotherly helping hand. This great act of humanitarianism deserves to be recognized and publicized. The leaders of the Virgin Islands are moral role models for every generation."